Populism
A Beginner's Guide

'The world is changing. Democracy is under threat. Simon Tormey's *Populism: A Beginner's Guide* provides a wonderfully sophisticated yet beautifully accessible guide to these changing times.'

**Matthew Flinders, Professor of Politics,
University of Sheffield**

'While we all think we know what populism means, if we dig a little deeper we find ourselves lost in definitional problems and ambiguities... Tormey navigates through these questions with admirable clarity and perception.'

**Saul Newman, Professor of Political Philosophy,
Flinders University**

'In this provocative, well-written new book, Tormey argues that populism can be both a threat to democratic values and process, but equally a means for the expansion of democracy... Tormey contends that we are misframing the problem by asking "what is to be done about populism?" when we should be asking "what has gone wrong with democracy?"'

**Duncan McDonnell, Professor of Politics,
Griffith University**

ONEWORLD BEGINNER'S GUIDES combine an original, inventive, and engaging approach with expert analysis on subjects ranging from art and history to religion and politics, and everything in-between. Innovative and affordable, books in the series are perfect for anyone curious about the way the world works and the big ideas of our time.

Populism
A Beginner's Guide

Simon Tormey

ONEWORLD

A Oneworld Book

First published by Oneworld Publications, 2019

ISBN 978-1-78607-613-7
eISBN 978-1-78607-614-4

Typeset by Geethik Technologies
Printed and bound in Great Britain by Clays Ltd, Elcograf S.p.A.

Oneworld Publications
10 Bloomsbury Street
London WC1B 3SR
England

Stay up to date with the latest books,
special offers, and exclusive content from
Oneworld with our newsletter

Sign up on our website
oneworld-publications.com

Contents

1

Introduction – why populism?

'A spectre is haunting the world – populism.' So begins one of the classic texts on the subject, echoing the dramatic opening of *The Communist Manifesto*: 'A spectre is haunting Europe – communism.' The warning, issued in the 1960s, referred to anti-colonial movements in the developing world, the farmers' parties of the US and assorted authoritarian movements.

Fear of new and powerful movements originating from the resentments of the people is far from as novel as a glance at many of the headlines since the election of Trump and the Brexit referendum in 2016 might suggest. On the contrary, it's a more or less permanent feature of commentary on the state of politics, whether at the national or the international level. Nevertheless, the events of 2016 were startling even for seasoned political commentators who might have seen it all before. It is these events that underpinned the latest wave of interest in populism and led to the suggestion that 2016 be regarded as the year populism 'exploded'.

2016 – the populism 'explosion'

Arguably, the first glimmer that something was afoot was neither Brexit nor the emergence of Trump but the election of

Rodrigo ('Rody') Duterte as President of the Philippines in May 2016. There seemed to be something quite novel in this result. Here was a politician who made no effort to hide his disdain for the rule of law and his support for the extrajudicial killing of drug dealers and petty criminals. Having campaigned on the promise to 'kill all' the country's criminals, in an interview with Al Jazeera he described the children killed in the course of his drug war as 'collateral damage'. 'In my country, there is no law that says I cannot threaten criminals,' he went on to explain. 'I do not care what the human rights guys say. I have a duty to preserve the generation. If it involves human rights, I don't give a shit. I have to strike fear.' He also threatened to turn his back on the United Nations and the USA in the search for new allies and an independent foreign policy, all the while promising to rid the Philippines of alien influences.

Duterte's election was closely followed by the UK's Brexit referendum in June 2016. Much to the surprise of the political class and most media commentary, the UK electorate voted, by a narrow margin, to leave the European Union (EU) after forty or so years of more-or-less unhappy membership of one of the largest, most powerful supra-national associations in the world. This was despite the campaigns of the major political parties that membership of the EU had bestowed enormous benefits, that economic catastrophe would follow from leaving, and that the UK would be left without friends in the event of a 'leave' vote. Fifty-two percent of those who voted turned their backs on 'Project Fear', as the Remain campaign was dubbed, opting for a leap into the political and economic unknown.

In the meantime, the American presidential campaign was in full flow. For much of the year it seemed that the Democrat candidate, Hillary Clinton, would win by a comfortable margin against Donald Trump, property developer, television celebrity and thorn in the side of various progressive causes, not least due to allegations of 'pussy grabbing' and disdain for a long list

RODRIGO DUTERTE

Rodrigo 'Rody' Duterte was elected President of the Philippines in 2016. He is a controversial figure, due to his uncompromising posture on drug dealers and petty criminals. According to *'You Can Die Any Time': Death Squad Killings in Mindanao*, a 2009 report from Human Rights Watch, as mayor of Davao, a major city in the south of the Philippines, Duterte presided over a policy of using execution squads to wipe out drug lords, resulting in hundreds, possibly thousands, of extrajudicial murders:

> Local activists say death squad killings of alleged drug dealers, petty criminals and street children in Davao City started sometime in the mid-1990s, during Duterte's second term as mayor. The group that claimed to be responsible for the killings was called *Suluguon sa Katawhan* ('Servants of the People') among other names but soon the media began referring to it as the Davao Death Squad (DDS). By mid-1997, local media had already attributed more than 60 unsolved murders to the group.

Duterte has admitted on more than one occasion to taking part in extrajudicial murders himself whilst an official in the region, on one occasion even telling the BBC that he had 'killed three men'. More generally, he is known for his rough and ready demeanour and frank views on matters of popular interest. He has also expressed a keenness to distance the Philippines from the US in order to pursue an independent foreign policy and permit the development of closer ties with China and other developing countries in the region.

of minorities. 'They're bringing drugs. They're bringing crime. They're rapists,' Trump famously said of Mexican immigrants in the June 2015 speech announcing his candidacy.

Trump had seemed barely to register as a viable candidate to the Republican Party, let alone to the wider electorate. His campaign was notable for its brutal, no-holds-barred approach. Supporters were urged to chant along to such memorable ditties as 'Lock Her Up!' and 'Build the Wall'. He promised to 'Make America Great Again' by bringing back lost manufacturing jobs, cutting corporation taxes, building the military and withdrawing from international agreements that didn't seem to serve narrow national interests. His campaign also threw away the rule book on democratic civility, with its bullying tone and barely-concealed threats of violence replacing the respectful discourse we usually associate with a democratic politics. Trump frequently said 'stupid people' were running the country, declared Senator John McCain was 'not a war hero', explaining at a July 2015 rally that he liked 'people who weren't captured' and, famously, at a rally in February 2016 encouraged his supporters to assault any protestors they spotted in the crowd: 'knock the crap out of them, would you? Seriously… I promise you, I will pay for the legal fees.'

As if the Brexit and Trump triumphs were not enough, the world braced itself for a further populist onslaught in Europe in 2017. Commentators were already wary of the direction the continent seemed to be taking, given the continued advance not only of far-right movements and parties, but the growing attractiveness of far-left parties such as *Syriza* in Greece and *Podemos* in Spain. Beppe Grillo's *Movimento 5 Stelle* ('Five Star Movement' (M5S)), though less easy to categorise as either left or right, promised a break from the pro-EU, pro-market policies of the Italian mainstream, themes associated with populist parties elsewhere in Europe.

There was much more to come, with a trio of elections due in key European countries: Holland, France and Germany. Whilst populist movements and parties had been on the rise across Europe for over a decade, with several notable successes, commentators nevertheless worried about both the scale of the advance and the prospects for the EU if one or more of the larger economies, such as France, Germany or Italy, succumbed to an anti-EU party. Surely the European mainstream would not go the way of the UK and the USA?

The Dutch general election was closely watched internationally, to see how Geert Wilders, leader of the main far-right party, the *Partij voor de Vrijheid* ('Party for Freedom' (PVV)) would fare. An easily recognisable figure, sporting a flamboyant platinum quiff, Wilders promised to 'de-Islamicise' Holland through reversing refugee- and immigrant-friendly policies that had seen an influx of new citizens from former colonies as well as the Middle East. In France, the presidential election scheduled for mid-year threatened to become a race between Marine Le Pen of the *Front National* (FN) and whichever candidate of the left or the centre-right could get their act together in time to oppose a party that, for all Le Pen's efforts at rebranding, is still widely seen as harbouring racists. Indeed, Steve Bannon, at an FN convention in March 2018, advised Le Pen and her followers to wear the label 'racist' as a badge of honour.

General elections scheduled for later in the year in Germany also promised to destabilise the established order. Angela Merkel, of the centre-right Christian Democrat Party (CDU), had

---

MARINE LE PEN

Marine Le Pen is a lawyer, and latterly leader of the French *Front National*, a far-right party created in 1972 and led for most of its existence by her father, Jean-Marie Le Pen. Marine Le Pen's niece (and Jean-Marie's granddaughter), Marion Maréchal-Le Pen, was also a national FN figurehead until she decided to take time out from politics in 2017. Marine Le Pen reached the second round of the 2017 French presidential election before being defeated by Emmanuel Macron. The main elements of the *Front National*'s programme included seeking withdrawal from the euro, and eventually the European Union. It also sought to reassert France's Christian heritage through a reduction of state support for multi-cultural initiatives, mosques and Islamic teaching. Le Pen also controversially aligns herself with Putin and Russia on issues of European security. Her long-term strategy, in order to find favour with the middle ground of the electorate, is to rid the FN of racism and anti-Semitism, a project that led her to rebrand the party as *Rassemblement National* ('National Rally') in the summer of 2018.

attracted criticism as well as plaudits from the international community for allowing more than one million refugees from the
war-torn Middle East into Germany. The path was open for a
breakthrough by the far-right *Alternative für Deutschland* (AfD)
party which, like its equivalents in Holland and France, promised
to wind back refugee-friendly policies in favour of a strongly
'nativist' stance seeking stronger borders and a greater sense of
national identity.

Populism panic

Early 2017 seemed to be a moment of 'populist revolution'.
Newspapers were full of alarmed commentary on the causes of
the crisis and what could be done to turn the tide back. It seemed
that the elite had failed, and an epoch of liberal cosmopolitanism
was coming to an end. Populism was no longer 'spectral'. It was a
viscerally real political crisis that threatened to dramatically alter
the shape and nature of our societies, and not for the better.

As it turned out, the anticipated overturning of establishment and mainstream political forces in Europe did not take
place. Wilders was defeated by Mark Rutte, who pragmatically
adapted to the rightward shift in Holland by acknowledging the
concerns of Wilders' supporters in relation to the 'Islamic threat'.
In France, the centre-left and centre-right predictably collapsed,
the first through division and splits, the latter through corruption and scandal. Into the vacuum stepped Emmanuel Macron,
a former merchant banker and economic adviser to the previous centre-left president, François Hollande. Macron created his
own political movement, *La République en Marche!* (literally 'the
Republic on the Move!'), in 2017. In a matter of months it had
gained just enough traction with the electorate to propel him
into the second-round contest with Le Pen and eventually to
a dramatic victory. Somewhat ironically, this was achieved not

by rejecting populism but by emphasising his own outsider status, the exhaustion of mainstream solutions and the need for a fresh start. In Germany the *Alternative für Deutschland* (AfD) made, as hotly anticipated, a breakthrough in the parliamentary elections but did not gain sufficient weight of numbers to topple the incumbent Chancellor, Angela Merkel. Merkel survived the scare but with her authority considerably diminished.

The European political class breathed a sigh of relief. A barely justified sigh, given other results around the continent. In the Austrian federal elections of 2017, the far-right Freedom Party (FPÖ) gained 26% of the vote and formed a governing coalition with the Austrian People's Party (ÖVP). The electorate continued to shift right, away from the centre and centre-left towards parties with strong anti-immigrant, anti-refugee and anti-Islam

GEERT WILDERS (PVV)

Geert Wilders is the leader of the PVV (People's Freedom Party) in Holland. A controversial figure with – as one memorable description puts it – the appearance of a 'Bond villain', he took up the baton for the critique of multiculturalism, immigration and the growing influence of Islam associated with Pim Fortuyn, leader of the Pim Fortuyn List (LPF), in 2002. Shortly after the LPF's creation Fortuyn was assassinated, leaving the way open for Wilders to become the leading figure on the Dutch far right. Like Fortuyn, Wilders argues that Holland is threatened by Islamisation due to its tolerance of minorities and how it has embraced multiculturalism. He has called for the Dutch state to reassert its liberal Christian heritage and to protect the culture and values of the West against Islam. 'Dutch values are based on Christianity, on Judaism, on humanism,' he told *USA Today*. 'Islam and freedom are not compatible.' Notwithstanding his defeat in the 2017 general election, Wilders maintains a high public profile both in Holland and abroad – when he is permitted entry. For example, in 2018 he spoke at a rally in support of Tommy Robinson, a spokesman for the far-right English Defence League (EDL) who had been imprisoned for contempt of court.

policies. A similar trend was witnessed in the Slovenian elections in 2018, when nationalist, anti-immigrant parties captured 29 of 90 seats in parliament. In the Italian general election of 2018, the two anti-establishment parties, Matteo Salvini's *Lega* and Grillo's M5S, emerged as the winners, leading to a ruling coalition of different populist tendencies. In the 2018 Hungarian election, Viktor Orbán, a rabble-rousing 'illiberal' nationalist, maintained his dominance over national politics with a third victory in a row. In the Swedish elections, the Swedish Democrats, with origins in neo-Nazi movements, enjoyed a 5% swing and an increase in their parliamentary presence to 62 seats. It is but the most prominent of several anti-immigrant parties making headway in the country, including the more militant Alternative for Sweden and the neo-Nazi Nordic Resistance Movement. Elsewhere, Jair Bolsonaro rose from relative obscurity to win the Brazilian presidential elections, notwithstanding his admiration for military dictatorship, deep social conservatism, openly expressed contempt for women ('I wouldn't rape you, you wouldn't deserve it,' he said to congresswoman Maria do Rosario), minorities (he told *Playboy* that he would be 'incapable of loving a homosexual son') and migrants (according to Open Democracy, he has called black activists 'animals' and called on them to 'go back to the zoo').

Support for outsider parties, anti-establishment parties, extreme or radical parties continues to grow, remorselessly, relentlessly. Hence the interest in populism, a concept that the media latched on to in 2016 to explain events. But what is populism? Why is it on the rise now? And what should we do about it?

2

What is populism? (and why does it seem so difficult to define?)

Populism seems to be very much on the rise. Indeed, as far as some commentators are concerned, populism 'exploded' in 2016, sparking the fear that we are entering new and uncharted political waters, an era of populist 'contagion' no less.

This presumes that we know what populism is. But do we? There seems to be little consensus as far as the academic literature is concerned. Margaret Canovan argues in her classic study that populism is a kind of political movement or ideology that places the idea of a unified people at the core of its vision. Cas Mudde influentially adjusted that view to argue that populism is not really a fully-fledged ideology, like socialism or liberalism, but a 'weak' ideology that augments other ideologies, such as authoritarianism or nationalism. Jan-Werner Müller identifies populism with an 'inner logic' that drives out pluralism and presages the onset of an intolerant regime injurious to liberal democracy. Ben Moffitt describes populism as more of a performative style, a politics associated with 'bad manners' and a brusque confrontational approach at odds with mainstream democratic approaches. By contrast Ernesto Laclau and Chantal Mouffe assert that since populism equates to a discourse of the people, it is fundamental to a properly democratic politics. Finally, media commentators such as Robert Peston and Steve Richards see populism as simply a proxy for 'outsider' forms of politics that challenge the elites.

Populism lends itself to a wide variety of definitions and uses. At one level there's nothing very unusual in political concepts being used in different ways in different contexts and for meanings to be contested. Indeed, there are concepts that are *so* debated that we have come to see them as 'essentially contested'. These are concepts such as liberty and equality, where how we define the concept reflects our own ethical and political commitments. As long as there is disagreement about how we should organise ourselves, there will be disagreement about how we frame and define the key concepts we use to describe the world as it is and as it *ought* to be.

This is not, however, applicable to the concept of populism. Populism doesn't lack conceptual clarity because it is essentially contested in the way terms such as liberty and equality are. With populism the nub of the issue is that historically very few movements or parties have described themselves as populist. Why?

What is clear in the various attempts at defining populism is the centrality of the idea of 'the people'. For populists 'the people' is the subject of politics, as opposed to any particular social class, ethnic grouping or nation. What motivates populists is some sense that the needs or interests of the people are at odds with the needs and interests of those who govern, whom commentators usually term 'the elites'. On the one hand, the elites are harming the people and it is this sense of injury that prompts populists to frame politics in confrontational or antagonistic terms. So far so good. On the other hand, this falls rather short of the kind of position we associate with ideologies. It's not telling us much about *why* we should prefer to speak about the people as opposed to some narrower group, or what is to be gained by confronting the elites. What we have is the description of a relationship: the people versus the elites. What's lacking are the basic co-ordinates we associate with political ideologies such as socialism, liberalism and conservatism; an account of how, ideally, we should live and what society should look like. This is because populism never blossomed into an intellectual credo or doctrine. There are some minor essays associated with the Russian peasant movements of the nineteenth century but there are few, if any, great texts or works of populism. There's nowhere to go if we want to find out more about what a 'populist society' would look like and why we should join a populist movement or party. There are no philosophers or great thinkers who espoused populism, or who made it into a consistent body of thought in the manner of Karl Marx (communism), John Stuart Mill (liberalism) or Edmund Burke (conservatism). There is very little to promote, to mobilise behind, or get excited about.

What this means is that populism has hardly ever been used as a *self-ascriptive* label, something one calls oneself. There are lots of parties that call themselves Marxist, liberal or socialist but as yet very few parties that call themselves 'populist'. Popular, yes but *populist*, no. Rather, it is a term that over the years has been applied to parties, movements and regimes that seem to share certain characteristics. Disputes over how we should define the concept, and how it should be applied, reflect differences of opinion concerning what these characteristics are and what weight we should give to certain features over others. These characteristics have been extracted from the small number of historical cases where either a movement or party *did* call itself populist or where the appellation 'populist' seemed for some reason to stick.

This is quite different to the situation that applies to other kinds of political movements and parties. Generally, we don't ascribe a term such as 'conservative' to parties or movements. We don't need to, because conservative parties and movements call themselves conservative. Since there aren't any self-proclaimed populist parties and movements, it's a term we use about others, sometimes with the aim of exposing the true intents and purposes lying behind an official designation: 'they may *say* they're nationalists but really they're populists'.

Not only is populism rarely a term of self-ascription, it's also a term that carries a negative connotation, which means the stakes are high when it comes to identifying groups and movements as populist. If populism is something bad, we should oppose it wherever we find it. We should do what we can to make sure it doesn't gain a foothold. We should fight back against populism. The need for clarity about what populism is and what it isn't goes beyond the familiar definitional dramas we find when we're trying to understand what a concept means. It will determine our orientation to one of the key developments going on around us.

A good place to start with this slippery definitional business is with the small number of cases that specialists in the field often refer to as baseline examples of populism. From these cases we should be able to extrapolate the key characteristics used to identify movements and parties as populist and see how they resonate with the contemporary movements and parties that have recently sparked interest in the concept.

The Russian *Narodniks*

Perhaps the classic case study for populism is the *Narodnik* movement, which began in Russia in the middle of the nineteenth century. *Narod* means 'people'; when added to terms like *Volya* or 'will' it gives the essence of what many want to capture in the term populism: the idea of a movement of the people as a whole, not just some part of it. The *Narodniks* were, for the most part, middle-class intellectuals who were swayed by the romantic depiction of peasant life in novels and poetry into believing that rural Russian culture and its traditions had to be preserved, indeed built on, to avoid the fate that had befallen peasants under capitalist development.

The peasants were simple toilers living a life uncontaminated by the excesses and decadence of city life. For the most part they were also God-fearing monarchists, but they also had a strong sense of their autonomy, reinforced by life in the '*Mir*' or commune, often hundreds of miles from the nearest city. Most peasants didn't possess the size of plot to be fully self-sufficient, so they worked together, sharing tools and livestock and distributing the proceeds of the sale of farming on a collective basis. To city-dwelling intellectuals this looked like a form of socialism, even communism, to be protected at all costs against the incursions of capitalism, wealthier landholders and the autocracy. Groups were created to promote *Narodnichechestvo* ('the way of the people') and peasant society was upheld as a solution for humanity's ills. Some of the groups were relatively peaceful, though there were also more militant political organisations, such as *Narodnaya Volya* ('The People's Will') that used violent means to confront autocracy.

The middle-class composition of the Russian populists reflects the fact that peasants were hardly in a position to advocate for themselves, even if they wanted to. Russia is a vast country, one which at that time was known for its poor communications. Most peasants were functionally illiterate and too busy trying to survive to be able to mobilise effectively for grander political ends. However, they enjoyed the sympathy of radicalised intellectuals, who saw in them an honesty and authenticity that could be developed into a distinctively Russian form of socialism. It was a romantic ideal that spoke to the idea of the 'soul' of Russia lying in the land and of those who tamed it for the benefit of the people.

The populists, who included the novelist Tolstoy, found themselves in competition with Marxists (called 'social democrats' at the time) for the affections of the radicalised elements of the population. Marx had argued that capitalist development would inevitably lead to the emergence of an industrialised working class, which would go on to outnumber the peasants and become their political leaders. Whereas Marxists urged the development of working-class consciousness and working-class organisation, the populists stressed the undifferentiated nature of the Russian people as a whole in their struggles against Tsarism and autocracy. Marx also stressed that the emancipation of the working class 'must be the task of the working class itself', implying that there was no need for leadership of the working class and therefore for the separation of representatives from those to be represented. However, given the state of the political consciousness of the peasant, the populists thought the people needed someone or some movement to represent them, to guide them, to save them. The virtuous, honest people would find a saviour from the rapacious conniving elites who saw in them merely a means for maintaining their exalted position and lives of luxury. The *Narodniks* thus created the template for a movement that understands the needs and interests of the people, that has a direct and unmediated relationship with the people and will therefore guide the people to the sunny uplands of a society in which present antagonisms are eliminated. For many, this is key to understanding the political dynamic at work in populism.

The farmers' parties of the United States of America

At around the same time as populism was emerging in Russia and seeking to establish itself as the main opposition to Tsarism, new and distinctive political parties were being created in the USA. Unlike Russia, the USA was already a democracy and it was therefore possible to create political parties legally and openly. The Republican and Democrat parties had both been set up earlier in the century to represent emerging interests and viewpoints. There was also a strong tradition of independent candidates standing for causes and issues that the main parties seemed to ignore.

Towards the end of the nineteenth century new parties were created to represent farmers and small landholders, who argued that their interests had largely been overlooked by metropolitan parties focusing on the needs of citizens in the new towns and cities. Their rhetoric focused on the 'common man' (often code for the common *white* man) protesting against the imposition of liberal and egalitarian values on the countryside. Nonetheless, there was also an undertow of resentment that the nation's new wealth and power seemed to barely trickle down to its impoverished parts, particularly in the South.

Further waves of populism crested intermittently over the course of the twentieth century. Occasionally they threatened to make an impact at the national level, as in the 1930s when the charismatic Huey Long created a deep impression on a sizeable part of the electorate. Long served as governor of Louisiana from 1928 to 1932 and then as Senator for the state until he was assassinated in 1935. A New Deal Democrat, he had developed a distinctive programme under the heading 'Share our Wealth', arguing that the southern poor had yet to benefit from economic advance and thus much greater redistribution was needed alongside the already extensive investment in infrastructure and services.

He was shortly followed by George Wallace, the firebrand governor of Alabama, who added a racial element to the discourse that chimed with southern, white working-class voters confronted with demands to desegregate schools and colleges. For a moment in the late 1960s and early 1970s it seemed as though populism would make a breakthrough on the national stage, only to be overwhelmed by the civil rights movement.

The sense of rural and agricultural people being ignored by the political mainstream was palpable, and the principal explanation for why these new parties came into being. There was also a strong sense of disenfranchisement, and of being ignored by a political establishment focused on rapidly-growing urban areas.

The new dimension was the emergence of fiery charismatic figures, such as Long and Wallace, who articulated the cause of the common man in blunt, approachable rhetoric that spoke directly to these constituencies and their concerns. Neither were fussed about the impact they would have on 'polite opinion'. Both anticipated what would become a key motif of populist leadership: no nonsense, plain speaking, with the implication that they were 'just like us'.

Latin American *caudillismo*

A third reference point for many of the classic studies of populism is the emergence of 'strongman' or *caudillo* regimes in Latin America over the course of the twentieth century. Here the focus is less on the characteristics or qualities possessed by the people and more about the political dynamic between governors and governed.

Spanish and Portuguese settler regimes struggled to maintain control over landless and indigenous populations and the nature of colonial conquest often left a bitter legacy of border and resource disputes that simmered on into the twentieth century. The colonial legacy of Latin America made for difficult to govern and often unruly societies with weak institutions but strong militaries. The response was the imposition of an ideology of nationhood to try to smooth the historical past and underpin the exercising of state power to prevent the break-up of nation states. Across the continent a similar pattern emerged: the imposition, usually through direct military and police power, of *caudillo* presidents and leaders seeking to unify the people and prevent disintegration.

The classic leader figure in populism studies is Argentina's Juan Perón, a former army officer who came to power after a military coup in 1943. This became the template for a raft of

similar regimes across the continent that claimed to represent and unify the people. The key claim was that the leader understood and knew what the country needed. That unity would be expressed in and through the leader, rather than through the constitution, the monarchy or the broader set of institutions underpinning the regime. As Perón himself noted, 'true democracy is where the government does what the people want and defends a single interest: that of the people'.

A true democracy is in this sense above the usual political fray. It's neither left nor right, terms that indicate a political orientation that divides the people rather than unites them. In a gesture that for many is typical of populism, it transcends the untidy terrain of politics altogether to generate a sense of the people being unified behind a figure who seeks an almost monarchical relationship with those being represented. Ideology is rejected in favour of a direct and unmediated relationship between the leader and the people they represent.

Three vignettes of past populist movements and leaders. They're certainly not the only ones we could refer to; there is always debate in populism studies concerning which regimes or movements represent the best examples of populism in action. But these examples crop up in almost every account of populism that seeks to extract a definition from case studies, which is the standard approach to trying to delineate what is unique or distinctive about populism when compared with other kinds of regime or movement. What characteristics do these movements and regimes display that in combination constitute populism?

In a nutshell, populism is a form or style of politics that:

- sees the fundamental antagonism in society as one between 'the people' (good) and 'the elites' (bad)
- frames the political context in terms of a 'crisis' that highlights the inadequacy of the political establishment

- offers a redemptive vision rather than a policy-driven, technocratic or problem-based approach
- centres on a charismatic figure who claims to possess extraordinary powers of leadership
- deploys a blunter, more confrontational, more direct use of language, or 'plain speaking'

How relevant then are these features for thinking about how populism looks today as opposed to previous centuries?

'The people' versus 'the elites'

The most distinctive feature of populist movements and parties is their penchant for dividing society into two antagonistic groups: the people on the one hand and the elites on the other. For some commentators, such as Ernesto Laclau, this is the only feature that differentiates populism from other styles of politics. However, this focus on the people is also one that causes a good deal of confusion. Why?

Insofar as we are looking at populism in democratic settings, we are discussing political systems where the people, the *demos* in Greek, is sovereign. Democracy was originally understood as *rule by the people*. In modern times, the people are frequently appealed to, as for example in the Constitution of the United States, which famously begins by intoning 'We the People of the United States, in Order to form a more perfect Union... do ordain and establish this Constitution for the United States of America'. It seems curious to identify an appeal to the people as something distinctive to populism. If the people are sovereign and in some sense the subject of a democratic politics, why should we associate the people with populism and not just democratic politics?

The answer lies in the distinctive characteristics of modern democracies. In ancient Athens all citizens were expected to undertake the common tasks necessary to the community, such as taking part in decision-making, holding public office and serving on juries. As a city-state, or *polis* (hence *politics*, the affairs of the *polis*), Athens had a small population, only a fraction of which – not including women, foreigners or slaves – was eligible to be considered as citizens. Only a small proportion of the overall population took part in politics and was able to do so only because it was sustained economically by the efforts of a much larger number of people who were not recognised as citizens.

With the emergence of much larger nation states in the early modern period, the shift to democratic systems came to imply a system of representation rather than direct participation by all citizens. Instead of democracy being defined in terms of the people governing themselves through direct decision-making, it became – in the famous words of Abraham Lincoln – government 'of the people, by the people, for the people', implying an important role for representation ('*for* the people').

With representation came political parties, to provide an organisational focus for those who shared a similar ideology, values or beliefs. During the eighteenth and nineteenth centuries political parties were created to defend particular interests, identities and ideologies. Liberals came together to form liberal parties, socialists to create socialist parties, Catholics to create Catholic parties.

Intrinsic to the evolution of modern representative systems is what political scientists call *pluralism*. This is the idea that complex societies are marked by significant differences of stance, opinion, identity and interests, encouraging the creation of different parties to represent these differences. One of the historic functions of elections has been to permit these different tendencies, identities and voices to compete in an open and tolerant environment, in which citizens can make their own choices as to which party or leader to vote for.

That's the theory. Whether it works like this in practice is a story to which we shall be returning. But the point is that democratic politics respects and builds on the *differences* between people, rather than one that sees the people as a homogenous mass to be represented by a single party or a single person.

The same is true when it comes to the nature of elites, the other side of the populist equation. Political scientists encourage an understanding of the elite as itself composed of different interests and needs and organisational forms. At the very least they want us to distinguish between *economic elites*, comprising banks, big business and the financial markets, and *political elites*, composed of the leaders and senior officials of political parties, ministerial officeholders and senior members of the civil service, to mention just a few.

Reducing this to the idea of a single 'elite' represents a simplification of a complex picture for the purpose of political point-scoring. This gets to the heart of another feature of populism, which is that it offers a radical *simplification* of social structures, including the elites. As we shall see, this is a constant theme in the critique of populism and the apparently irresponsible, immature approach it takes to governance.

Lastly we need to touch on the nature of political *antagonism* under democratic conditions. Historically, political parties' great advantage has been that they have ensured that major divisions in society have been represented in the legislature. Socialists and liberals have their own political parties, and so where relevant, do Protestants and Catholics. And so on through the many positions and identities in complex modern settings. This means that divisions in society that might conceivably become disruptive find an outlet in the system of governance. It has ensured that minority voices are heard, whilst at the same time enshrining the principle of majority rule or 'majoritarianism' that lies at the heart of representative democracy.

Populism turns all this on its head, by insisting on the essential *unity* of the people in their struggle with elites. As Jan-Werner

Müller puts it, populism equates to 'a particular moralistic imagination of politics, a way of perceiving the political world that sets a morally pure and fully unified – but, ultimately fictional – people against elites who are deemed corrupt or in some other way morally inferior'. This goes well beyond the kind of majoritarian logic we are used to in representative democracy towards a stance that many commentators see as incipiently totalitarian, where all differences between individuals are erased in favour of a 'monist' understanding of the collective. This causes concern among those for whom democracy is as much about the protection of minorities as it is about respecting the wishes of the majority. Populism is, for this reason, often portrayed as bullying, intolerant and a danger to hard-won minority rights.

Never let a good crisis go to waste

Without crisis there is little chance of populism gaining traction. Populism sets the people against the elites or the governing class, which implies the existence of a crisis as far as the relationship between those who represent and those who are represented is concerned.

Populism is an unusual or extraordinary form of politics. It gains a foothold where 'normal' politics fails to provide solutions to the problems that concern or animate citizens. People look beyond the usual menu of choices, towards a leader or parties that provide a more radical analysis that speaks to these concerns and promises to resolve them.

The discussion of the *Narodniks* showed that Russian populism came about under conditions of autocracy. Lacking any legal outlet for political views that challenged the regime, activists – understandably – used the language of the people versus the ruling elite to generate political momentum. Change had to come from outside or beyond the monarchy. Indifferent autocratic rule, bad harvests and an enduring question mark over a particular way of life made a useful base for populists to build on.

In the USA the sense of crisis was precipitated by the hardship endured by small farmers, shopkeepers, the poor and the marginalised, who thought their needs and interests were ignored by the political mainstream. They created their own parties and used the language of the people to forge a common cause with others 'doing it tough'. This contrasts with Latin America, where politics often takes place against the background of opposition and dissent (not least by excluded elements of the population), leading to an atmosphere of crises of identity, of living standards, of nationhood and collective survival. This is rich soil for populism to thrive in.

Fast forward to recent years and we encounter parties and outsider figures seeking to generate discontent with the performance of those who govern. The far right has made rapid progress over the past two decades in Europe by provoking a sense of cultural crisis in relation to immigration, the influx of refugees and fear of a Muslim minority growing to such an extent that it challenges the dominant Christian ethos of European society. The commitment of European elites to free movement of people, multiculturalism and a cosmopolitan sensibility has put them sharply at odds with the idea of promoting and protecting distinct cultural and social identities. Much of continental Europe is preoccupied with the rapid influx of refugees from the Middle East and North Africa, and from a perception of existential threat to their own culture and traditions posed by the 'Islamisation' of Europe. In the UK, the vote in favour of Brexit stemmed in large measure from the view that public services had been 'swamped' by millions of immigrants from eastern Europe and beyond. Nigel Farage added fuel to the fire by launching a poster supposedly representing thousands of Turkish people queuing up for access to Britain. The photograph he used was actually of refugees fleeing the war zone in Syria, underlining the tawdriness of the stunt.

Nearer the present, the global financial crisis brought the competence of the elites into question. Many countries suffered during the recession, as austerity policies hit the poor and widened the gulf between the haves and have-nots. In his inauguration speech Donald Trump made great play of the crisis afflicting American manufacturing industry and, by extension, working-class people when he touched on the theme of 'American carnage', dramatically raising the political stakes for his own term of office.

Populism is an *effect* of crisis but it can also be a *cause* of it. Populist politicians understand that their pitch will gain traction only if people believe there is a crisis requiring a radical change of course, a new politics and new leadership. This helps explain the character and tone of populist politics, which often seeks to highlight some alleged deficiency, using distorting statistics and dramatic language and imagery to heighten the sense that urgent action is needed – action that the elites are unable or unwilling to deliver. Populists understand that in the absence of crisis we can expect the political system to revert to its usual undramatic character, with citizens choosing who should represent them from the usual menu. Only impending disaster that the existing leadership cannot avert will see citizens reject the mainstream in favour of an outsider.

Redemptive versus humdrum politics

If populism thrives on a sense of crisis, and indeed requires the perception of crisis to gain traction, this is because it offers a redemptive vision, as opposed to the 'politics as usual' approach favoured by the political mainstream: only they can save the people from a calamity or fate that otherwise threatens the people's prosperity, security and, perhaps, very existence.

The Russian populist movement was inspired by the idea of saving Russia from the fate that had befallen the west. Industrialisation and urbanisation led, so it was argued, to godlessness, consumerism and decadence. The people had to be saved from themselves. This meant the creation of a movement that would resist westernisation and promote the simple nobility of the peasant and the *Mir* or communal style of life. Similar sentiments, differently phrased, underpinned the emergence of populism in the USA. Again, the simplicity and nobility of rural life was contrasted with the heady cocktail of temptations represented by life in emerging towns and cities. In Latin America, populist movements impressed the existential threat of lawlessness and the collapse of the integrity of the nation on audiences faced with challenges from without in the form of regional rivalry and from within in the form of political division, social unrest and economic failure.

Similar themes are expressed by today's politicians. Trump's election campaign slogan 'Make America Great Again' emphasised another dimension of the populist pitch: a nostalgia for a lost world, a lost society, a society that needs to be recovered – or recreated – to recuperate a sense of collective order and harmony. In Europe the dominant theme concerns the threat to national identity and, more broadly, to what is held to be distinctive to European civilisation – as opposed, supposedly, to other cultures such as Islam – human rights, free speech and religious toleration. It seeks a return to the post-Westphalian world of nation states enjoying sovereignty and control over borders, co-operating when needed to promote collective security. Europe needs to turn its back on cosmopolitanism, globalisation and open borders and look after its own.

This redemptive style of politics, this promise to save the people, is in marked contrast to the discourse of mainstream democratic politics, which usually rotates around the nitty-gritty of ensuring that people have somewhere to live, somewhere to work and somewhere for their children to be educated. Moreover, democratic politics is often characterised by a 'technocratic' style of governance, in a framework that is acknowledged to be composed of multiple stakeholders, a high level of complexity, multi-level governance and varying and competing interests. It's a politics that seeks 'optimal outcomes', 'value for money' and 'consensus', as opposed to spectacular 'wins', to paraphrase Trump. Democratic politics rotates around the necessity for negotiation, compromise, give-and-take, not least because electoral arithmetic often means that a governing party needs a certain degree of co-operation from other parties, including opposition parties and interests, to keep the show on the road. This can result in outcomes that are the result of compromise and negotiation rather than a singularity of purpose or vision. Or 'fudge' as it is disparagingly known. All too often this can come across as grey politics for grey folks in grey suits.

Populism rejects this, in favour of a radically simplified, redemptive vision of a people reborn and unchained from the complexity and divisions that otherwise engulf it. It presents itself as a direct, exciting, uplifting style of politics; a refreshing break from the often highly technical forms of legislation that are the nitty-gritty of democratic policymaking. It's a politics that speaks directly to our emotions, to our deepest fears and to our deepest hopes. As film directors know, audiences like clarity of purpose. They like clearly-badged goodies and baddies and they like cathartic happy endings. Populism is to politics what Hollywood is to the movies. It sets the humdrum and routine to one side, in favour of the epic and spectacular: 'Let's Build a Big, Beautiful Wall!'

Take me to your leader

It's hardly surprising that a charismatic leader is a key feature of populism: Perón, Le Pen, Trump, Wilders; the list is long.

But there are exceptions. Russian populism not only lacked charismatic figures, it also lacked leaders with a genuine connection to those they were seeking to lead. It was largely an intellectual exercise, punctuated by episodes of violence and drama, as lone wolves sought to assassinate members of the ruling class, never a true mobilisation. In America, populism threw up spokespeople but few heavyweight figures with the ability to mobilise people effectively; Huey Long and George Wallace being perhaps the notable exceptions. Populist *candidates* such as Pat Buchanan and Ross Perot have come and gone but the resilience of the two-party system makes it difficult for independent candidates to gain national traction. The Tea Party provided the semblance of significant rallying to a populist cause but was always dogged by accusations that it was more AstroTurf than grass roots.

By contrast, Latin America offers many examples of strongmen who fit the template of the charismatic leader: Perón, Chávez, Castro, Guevara, Ortega and, most recently, Bolsonaro. We may debate whether the movements they led or are associated with are populist but there's no doubting that *caudillismo* runs deep in the history of the region. In contemporary politics, it is easier to identify figures who match the description. Trump is already the classic (and certainly the most discussed) example but others exemplify the issues just as clearly. Jean-Marie Le Pen, former leader of the French *Front National* (now the National Rally) illustrates the nature of the populist leader in many respects; trading on a heady mix of bluster, criticism of elites, simplistic rhetoric and dubious views. Le Pen also illustrates the nature of the relationship between the populist leader and the party. In voters' minds, the *Front National* became strongly identified with Le Pen; unsurprisingly, given that he led the party from 1972 until 2011. So implanted is the association that it was similarly unsurprising when his daughter, Marine Le Pen, took over as leader, and indeed when his granddaughter (and Marine's niece)

Marion Maréchal-Le Pen rose to prominence as a FN politician at a precociously young age.

Rather than the leader serving the party, populist parties often appear to exist as vehicles for the advance of a particular politician or family. Contrast this situation with well-established mainstream democratic political parties, such as the Democrats in the USA, the Conservatives in the UK or the Christian Social Union (CSU) in Germany. There, the leader is democratically accountable to their deputies, the party membership and occasionally, directly to their citizens. The party existed before the leader and will continue to exist once the leader has moved on, retired or been deposed. The party is the repository of the values, ideology and programme with which people identify; the leader is a figurehead and perhaps the key to its electoral fortunes. But the party can and will survive the coming and going of any particular leader.

This sense of the party having primacy over the leader is often weaker in populist parties or movements. Since it is usually the *leader* who promises redemption, the promised land, salvation from crisis, populism tends to be a more *personal* style of politics, notwithstanding the 'presidentialisation' of politics that is noticeable in the political mainstream as well as at the margins. Voters are asked to buy into the exceptional qualities of an individual person, so it stands to reason that the leader has a particularly privileged place in the party. The populist leader is omniscient, far-sighted, inspirational; the fount of the movement, whose rationale often appears to be to deliver that person to power.

Leaders are important, but are they crucial in terms of defining populism? In contemporary politics, there is some ambivalence concerning just how important. Certainly, the news media have no difficulty in continuing to term certain political parties populist, even in the absence of a clear leader in the Trump or Le Pen mould. *Podemos*, created in 2014 by radical democrats in

Spain, is often termed populist but it was set up, and in the early days led by, a triumvirate (Pablo Iglesias, Íñigo Errejón and Juan Carlos Monedero). AfD had two leaders, one of whom immediately resigned after the general election but without, it seems, diminishing their appeal. Italy's Five Star Movement was set up by a charismatic figure, Beppe Grillo, though he insists that he is not the leader and indeed, he has never held elected office.

The situation is a little more complex than at first glance. It's probably more accurate to note that populism lends itself to a particular *kind* of leadership and a particular kind of discourse. Populist parties and movements can exist and succeed where they lack a charismatic or clearly identifiable figure in the manner of the Le Pens. Many of Europe's far-right parties have survived the coming and going of leaders without dulling their appeal

PODEMOS (WE CAN)

Podemos is a Spanish left-wing political party created in 2014 after the citizen protests of 15 May 2011 (popularly known as #15M). The protests were sparked by the imposition of austerity measures in the wake of the financial crash, bringing more than six million citizens on to the streets to occupy squares and public places. *Podemos* was created to give an electoral focus to citizens' demands. Its leaders include Pablo Iglesias and Íñigo Errejón, both lecturers at the Complutense University in Madrid. The party made an immediate breakthrough in the European elections of 2014, winning 9% of the vote and five seats in the European Parliament. In the Spanish general elections of 2016 and 2017 it polled around 20% of the popular vote, disrupting the two-party system that had been in evidence since Spain's transition to democracy in the 1970s. *Podemos* stands for greater public participation in decision-making, redistributive social policies and an end to the corruption and cronyism that has marked Spanish political culture. It is also strongly internationalist and an advocate of the reform of the EU. Ada Colau and Manuela Carmena, political figures allied to *Podemos* and #15M, were elected mayors of Barcelona and Madrid in 2015.

to electorates. But it might also be that these far-right parties, in particular those in Scandinavia, are not really populist. They might have a populist discourse (the people versus the elites, etc.) but they lack certain qualities that, for example, the National Rally displays.

Controversies of this kind are the stock in trade of the ongoing debates in political science concerning how we should define populism and whether (for example) far-right parties are by definition populist, or just more likely to become populist. For commentators such as Jan-Werner Müller the larger point about populism is that it seeks a direct or unmediated connection to the people. It doesn't recognise pluralism as an intrinsic and desirable feature of democratic governance. It is impatient and often intolerant of systems of representation based on pluralism and respect for the views and opinions of others. Why go through the motions of tolerating these different and competing political forces when you have a *direct and immediate connection* to the people, when you understand their deepest needs and desires? Pluralism and the system of competition of parties and interest groups is just so much stuff getting in the way of this visceral bond, to paraphrase Marine Le Pen. For populism the task is the simplification of the political, its reduction to a relationship built on a monochrome understanding of representation. The leader represents the people; the people see their leader as distinctive and special. This is, at one level, presidentialism *in extremis*, a secularised translation of monarchy for a hyper-mediatised age.

Incivility as a weapon of politics

Populism is an *extraordinary* form of politics. Extraordinary in the sense that it rejects the ordinary as complicit in the continuation of an unbearable state of affairs; the subjugation of the people by villainous elites. Populism is an emotive politics. It is a politics of exasperation at the state of the world. It is therefore one that has little hesitation resorting to styles and forms of behaviour that startle, shock and confront.

This is, it must be said, more an emerging feature of contemporary populism than one particularly marked in our foundation cases. With regard to the Russian populists, as a variety of romantic anti-capitalism, the discourse is better characterised as lyrical, nostalgic and just a little patronising, not least towards the modest Russian peasant, the object of their affections. In the USA, the populist tone was of righteous indignation, bordering on contempt for the faraway metropolitan figures who had failed the honest toilers in the countryside. In Latin America, it is a discourse marked by fiery vitriol on the one hand and inflated redemptive promises on the other.

Little hint here of what will become one of the hallmarks of contemporary populist politics: 'bad manners', as Ben Moffitt puts it. But even here we can see that populism rejects the humdrum, routine and everyday business of attending to politics as usual. In each case we see that this is politics as mission, as salvation, rather than as the matter of ensuring that public services are provided, the trains run on time and waste is collected. Populism is a heroic undertaking, not a politics-as-usual affair. This requires an expansive, ambitious style of discourse addressing the existential needs of the people and the nation. Currently, we see this grand narrative joined with the bullying tone that many now associate with populism, in particular with people such as Duterte, Trump, Farage, Bolsonaro and Pauline Hanson, founder of the One Nation Party and scourge of the multicultural left in Australia.

Perhaps the most shocking aspect of Trump's rapid rise to power was the contempt he displayed first towards his opponents in the Republican Party and then towards Hillary Clinton. Typical was Trump's leading of the chorus of 'Lock Her Up!' at his campaign rallies. It is difficult to find many parallels in contemporary democratic discourse for the sheer ugliness and incivility Trump displayed in his presidential campaign. The examples of his boor-ish behaviour are multiple, from his repeated finger-pointing and cries of 'fake news' to assembled news reporters, to his belittling of rivals, such as calling the North Korean leader Kim Jong-un 'rocket man'. Everywhere he goes, Trump seems to cause offence, anger and dismay.

Incivility is perhaps a rather mild term, given the direction that contemporary populist leaders seem to be heading. Populism often uses a language more tuned to war or conflict than reason-able democratic debate. The Le Pens' language is full of betrayal, of 'traitors', 'cheats' and 'assassins'. In her 2017 presidential cam-paign, Marine Le Pen insisted that the choice facing the French people was between someone who understood the perils facing the nation (her) and one who was complicit in the growing feel-ings of insecurity, fear and loathing that marked French society (Macron). The line between respectful critique, of the kind famil-iar in democratic contexts, and the smearing of opponents is one populists cross with facility.

The same can be said for a host of others across Europe. Wilders is a well-known critic of Islam, who has talked about banning the Qur'an and closing mosques in the Netherlands. He is a frequent critic of the political class in his own country, accus-ing them of lacking the 'political guts' and 'feeling of urgency' to resist the Islamification of the country. In Hungary, Orbán constantly rails against refugees and immigrants, as well as weak-kneed members of Parliament afraid of defending the national interest.

The point is that the language is at best blunt, but often vicious and hateful. Little wonder that the rise of populist polit-icians has been accompanied by a rise in hate crimes against those who form the object of their critique. This includes not just ordi-nary members of the public marked by the colour of their skin or the clothes they wear, but also by members of the contemp-tuous elites who stand in the way of redemption. Many British

MPs have complained about how Brexit has altered the tone of public life and made their work more precarious, by giving an enhanced platform to politicians such as Nigel Farage, who made his name pointing to the failings of politics and politicians in the EU and the UK. When Jo Cox, a British Labour MP who vocally and publicly stood up for the rights of immigrants and refugees, was murdered by a neo-fascist Brexit supporter, this tragedy was, it is argued, testimony to the coarsening of public life and the ramping up of the stakes of political debate. Jo Cox paid the ultimate price for her humanitarian stance in the face of the anti-immigrant onslaught.

Populism is an unusual concept. It doesn't conform to the characteristics usually associated with ideologies or 'isms'. If it is an ideology, it is a weak or thin one; not a well-developed ideology with a basis in a sophisticated doctrine, such as Marxism, but a kind of sentiment elevated to a political practice or worldview: power to the people, not the elites. Alternatively, Müller (for example) urges that we should see populism as possessing an 'inner logic', a certain way of thinking about how and for whom politics functions, which in turn may or may not reveal some malign tendency.

For the most part, the idea of populism as a syndrome marked by certain traits and characteristics is closer to how many specialists, as well as many in the media, see it. It also captures the sense many commentators seek to explore of populism as a temporal event appearing at a particular juncture, hence the frequent references to the populist explosion, the populist moment and so on. This reinforces the idea of populism as something that *happens*, rather than just a *type* of politics, party, movement, ideology or regime. Insofar as it is a type of politics, I've tried to capture the essence of populism in this set of characteristics. It is not definitive by any means. There are those who will insist that a charismatic leader is much less significant than the use of one kind of discourse (the people versus the elites). Others will feel that the stylistic or performative aspects of populism ('bad manners', coarsening of language, etc.) count for less than the substantive content of the populist claim: the elites have let us down and need to be challenged from without. The point is not to close this debate by insisting on a pristine definition of populism but rather to give a sense of how populism is used by specialists in political science and media commentary.

Perhaps because of these idiosyncrasies, we should not overlook the fact that the concept of populism also has its detractors, those who think that it is flawed in some way. It's a contentious term and one that arouses suspicion almost every time it is used and in whatever context. Before leaving behind my attempt to define populism it will be useful to pause for a moment to consider some objections to populism.

Problems with populism – ahistorical and descriptive?

Populism is a concept that refers to a set of characteristics. It has no lineage that we can use to trace its origins. Or if it has, it is a very haphazard one. This makes populism a very different 'ism' to ideologies such as Marxism or liberalism. Marxism began with Marx; what makes a movement or a party Marxist is that it identifies with his intellectual legacy, analysis and prescriptions. Those wanting to know more about the history of Marxism can follow the trajectory of ideas and practice of those who called themselves Marxist. Since populism doesn't have adherents, this kind of operation is closed. Populism lacks a 'home', a set of agreed reference points that constitute it as an ideology, a set of beliefs or mobilising viewpoint. As a result, populism almost becomes whatever anyone wants to make of it. Any discussion of whether a certain party movement or leader is or is not populist requires a definition of what the author means by populism. Even by the normal standard of debates in politics, this degree of reflexivity is unusual.

This implies that the rationale of the concept of populism is less about tracing the flow of intellectual inheritance and more about assembling cases among which – notwithstanding significant differences – there seem to be some important similarities, even if only weakly descriptive. This, some have argued, is not very good history, and pretty thin political sociology. It's not difficult to see why the objection has arisen. Russian peasant movements, American farmers' parties, Latin American *caudillo* are very different political phenomena, located in very different intellectual and political terrain, underpinned by a multitude of very different political actors and issues. What links them? Some sort of critique of the way matters are run by reference to the needs of the people, which have otherwise been ignored or overlooked by their representatives? Nothing very unusual in that. Indeed, we could turn the issue around and ask where *haven't* we seen similar sorts of claims arise, with the adjacent claim that some movement or leader has the answer to our collective problems. Outsider movements and figures are part of the rich tapestry of political life the world over and feature, more or less continuously, in the evolution of political systems.

If the objection is that noisy outsider movements are new to democratic systems such as the UK's, then we need to remind ourselves of the great heritage of rumbustious anti-establishment movements and leaders that marks British history, from the medieval heretics, the Movement of the Free Spirit, to the Diggers, the Levellers, Winstanley, Godwin, Shelley, the Chartists. The list goes on. The same is true for most political systems that have evolved into democracies. Where we find an establishment or elites, we invariably find outsiders and anti-elite groups, movements and claims. We could go further and note that the democratic revolution that started in the early modern period can be understood in terms of successive waves of 'outsiders' criticising the power and privilege of elites in the name of greater democratic engagement and participation. Without outsiders, protests and social movements challenging elites we get stasis, not progress, in terms of the evolution of democratic systems.

There seems to be some justification for the charge that populism lacks a proper anchor in a definite tradition of thought or practice. Even researchers in populism studies recognise that there is something idiosyncratic (or perhaps distinctive) about the concept of populism. It's part of what makes the concept interesting and stimulates debate and criticism, but it also helps explain why these debates often seem to get bogged down in definitional battles. If these battles are not unique to populism, they certainly seem to feature larger in these debates than in many others in political science.

Indifferent to beliefs and values?

One of the most commented-on features of populism is that it can appear indifferent to differences of ideology, belief and values. The Russian populist movement was a left-wing movement of a socialistic kind. The American populist movements were often libertarian and conservative in their instincts but Huey Long, to take one prominent example, was a New Deal Democrat. Latin American regimes described as populist have been right-wing, left-wing, communist, and centrist, such as Perón's.

Today, Trump, Farage and Le Pen are often described as populists but increasingly we find that radical non-mainstream figures on the left, such as Bernie Sanders, Pablo Iglesias, Jean-Luc Mélenchon (leader of *La France Insoumise* ('France Unbowed')) and Alexis Tsipras, are also described as populist, particularly by the media, who have got themselves in a frenzy about the rise of outsider parties and figures. This is despite the fact that the goals of right-wing figures such as Trump and Le Pen are quite different from those of Iglesias and Tsipras. The former are nativist, anti-immigrant and anti-cosmopolitan; the latter are internationalist, socialist and egalitarian. How has the way these people pursue their objectives come to be considered more significant than their very different agendas?

The issue relates to the origins of the concept of populism in political science. Comparative politics is, as the label suggests, about comparing features, in particular the features shared by political parties, movements, electoral systems and legislatures. It's an approach more interested in characteristics than the professed aims, goals or philosophy of a movement or party. This implies that what unites people as otherwise diverse as Trump, Farage, Iglesias and Tsipras is more important than what divides them. It doesn't matter that far-right populists can be (borderline) racists and nativists and that left populists profess egalitarianism and inclusivity. Some characteristic, some inner logic or weak ideology, unites them.

There are several kinds of objection to this flattening of otherwise quite different movements and phenomena. First, given that most populism movements and parties come from the political right (Trump, UKIP, the National Rally, AfD, etc.), there's a − perhaps natural − tendency to extrapolate from them. Shouty leaders, bad manners, threats to institutions such as the press and media; we see the same behaviours repeated and repeated on the right. But they are much less evident on the left. Tsipras, Iglesias, Sanders: excitable? Yes. Obnoxious, threatening, malignant? Not really. We could argue that 'it's just a matter of opinion' but the comparison seems less than compelling, certainly at first glance. Are these left movements really a threat to civil society and democratic institutions? Some will argue the toss but the evidence is thin. Extrapolations often work, but this piece of elastic has been stretched to the point where we lose touch with the value of the initial analysis: that populism means some sort of break with 'normal' or mainstream politics.

This leads to a second point – the moral equivalence between the far right, which might seek to victimise minorities and close debate, and the far left, which might seek to remedy injustice, provide welfare and clean up the system of governance. We are often urged to resist or reject populism on grounds that it is unreasonable, extreme or a danger to minorities, so the stakes are high. The efforts of writers on populism can sometimes seem more like an exercise in tethering noisy or troublesome movements to avoid having to engage with substantive political claims. This is indeed one claim: outsider movements are all the same; for example, they're all outside the mainstream. But the alleged similarity is a concern for those who think we should judge movements and parties not only in terms of how they *appear* but also in terms of what they are seeking to *achieve*, and how they are going to realise their aims. Take that away and we are left with a conservative-sounding analysis that privileges the status quo because it is less noisy, troublesome and question-begging than outsider politics.

An alibi for the performance of elites?

As a concept, populism describes a particular kind of politics, but it doesn't tell us much about *why* this particular kind of politics arises. This is alluded to in a piece in *The National Interest*, written by Francis Fukuyama, a conservative commentator who notes that: 'Populism is the label that political elites attach to policies supported by ordinary citizens that they [that is, the elites] don't like.' What he is getting at is the rather subtle role that the concept of populism can play in averting our gaze from the political dynamic at work in many of our societies. We've already discussed the issue of what differentiates figures such as Trump and Iglesias but it is worth reminding ourselves what undoubtedly unites them: they are critical of the performance of elites. Elites, they claim, have let us down. They have inflicted policies that have led to outsourcing of jobs, financial catastrophe, evictions, recession and austerity. And all the while looking after themselves and their client groups.

By labelling this critique 'populist', commentators contain it and make it sound unreasonable and irrational. Populism evokes negative thoughts: fear of the mob, incivility, emotive politics, attacks on minorities and institutions. In this sense, populism provides a perfect alibi for elites. It deflects the critique back on to those offering it, suggesting that we need to do everything possible to ensure that the populist contagion does not spread, so that the elites can sleep untroubled.

Fukuyama's point is important. It broadly highlights a feature of political language: the terms we use carry an ideological inflection of which we may be unaware. Populism is not, in this sense, an innocent, value-free, concept. Very few concepts in the lexicon of politics are. Yet critics such as Fukuyama detect something fishy at work here, something that points towards the ideological usage of a term to support and sustain the elites and the world they have created.

We have been here before. In the 1940s and 1950s the concept of totalitarianism was popularised to provide a handy shorthand for far-right and far-left regimes such as Germany under Hitler and the Soviet Union under Stalin. Like populism, totalitarianism is an 'ism' without adherents, in the sense that no one called themselves a 'totalitarian'. In its classic formulation in the work of Carl Friedrich and Zbigniew Brzezinski, totalitarianism is a 'syndrome' based on a list of 'interrelated traits and characteristics'. Much like scholars describe populism. Apparently neutral and objective in terms of the analysis, the concept quickly came under attack from specialists concerned about the manner by which the concept collapsed vital differences between these regimes in terms of ideology and belief system. They also expressed their concern that it would become a weapon in the hands of ideologists, a 'boo word', as Frederic Fleron put it, to describe 'boo regimes'.

These objections were well borne out in practice. To take one notable example, Jeane Kirkpatrick, foreign policy adviser to Ronald Reagan, argued that 'totalitarian' should be used against any regime that stood in the way of the USA's interests: good regimes were to be termed 'authoritarian' and bad ones 'totalitarian'. She understood the power of words. Apply the term 'totalitarian' to a country and public opinion could more easily be convinced that the USA should isolate it and seek regime change: 'Why, they're just the same as those communists and Nazis.' Many of the concerns articulated in the 1960s and 1970s about totalitarianism resonate with today's concerns about the concept of populism: 'Iglesias? He's just as bad as those other extremists in Europe. Better do what we can to make sure he doesn't win.'

There's a suspicion that behind the studious façade the concept of populism is doing valuable work for elites, drawing the eye from the underlying causes for the rise of outsider parties and movements to some safe spot where elites look like the victims of unreasonable, if not anti-democratic, forces. It neutralises the critique of outsiders and radicals by tethering them to parties and movements that might well be unreasonable and anti-democratic. In short, populism has become a powerful tool in the ideological war of words between those defending the status quo and those seeking change.

Conclusion

We might be forgiven for thinking it is not worth the bother of seeking clarity about what populism means and how we can use it. Given the problems of the concept, it's an understandable concern. But the concept is not going to go away because criticisms have been levelled at it. This is not how concepts in political discourse work. Populism is a term that many, both in academic circles and the media, find useful.

With this in mind, I have gathered the various elements that commentators use to develop an understanding of populism with an eye to seeing how the concept functions, to what ends, and to what purposes. This is not to say there are no important variations between how those using it define and deploy the concept. As I noted at the outset, there are important differences, not least when it comes to assessing the degree to which populism is a threat to democracy. But by and large, the characteristics assembled here broadly capture how the concept of populism is used by academics and political commentators.

I've also tried to give a sense of why not everyone following contemporary developments is happy with the term. There are significant criticisms of how populism has been defined and its overall utility for political analysis. We need to bear these in mind as we come to think about the nature of the populist contagion that many believe has engulfed democratic societies. In the next chapter, I will focus on this contemporary setting and ask whether, and to what extent, what we are seeing is consistent with the populist account of democratic crisis, or whether there might be some other more useful framing for what is going on. In short: why populism and why now?

3
Why now? Explaining the populist insurgency

Until quite recently populism seemed a rather obscure topic. Debate about what constituted populism and why it appeared in particular places and at particular times was confined to a sub-field of political science: 'populism studies'. As we have seen in the previous chapter, a characteristic of the sub-field is the weighing and sifting of historical cases, often of a fairly esoteric kind, in the search for connections between movements and causes that might otherwise have little in common.

This changed in 2016. With the Brexit referendum and the election of Donald Trump, populism became a topic of wide public interest. The world wanted to know about populism; in particular why there seemed to be such an upsurge of outsider movements and figures at this particular moment. What has led to the growth of outsider figures and parties committed to undermining or challenging the status quo? Why have millions of citizens in otherwise peaceful, relatively stable and affluent societies turned their backs on mainstream political parties and elite politics?

Before turning to different explanations for recent developments we should perhaps remind ourselves that posing the matter in these terms ('why the sudden upsurge of populism?') does not obviate the point that radical, and in particular far-right, politics has been in the ascendancy for the past couple of decades in many advanced democracies. When we look at Europe, we see that parties such as the National Rally, UKIP, the *Lega Nord* (now *Lega*) and the Austrian Freedom Party have been making steady progress since the early 1990s. Figures such as Geert Wilders, Viktor Orbán and Nigel Farage have been around just as long, if not longer. The fact that interest in populism and radical politics spiked in 2016 should not obscure the point that these forms and styles of politics have been around for decades. If anything, 2016 represents a coming of age, a maturing of trends and tendencies, rather than an unforeseen or dramatic efflorescence. Nonetheless, judging by the number of books, column inches, television debates and conferences devoted to populism, it's certainly the case that *interest* in populism exploded in 2016.

In this chapter we will look at the two main theories behind the upsurge of populist parties and movements. The first is often termed *economic grievance* theory, which focuses on the impact of recession and austerity. The second is *cultural grievance* theory, which focuses on issues of the threat to identity and belonging posed by migration. Most accounts of populism, both in academic literature and the media, focus on these theories. We also need to think, however, about longer-range sociological changes, which don't always feature in accounts of why populism has become so implanted in our political systems. We need to look at themes of 'post-democracy', political decadence, individualisation, the collapse of authority and the impact of digital technology to understand the appeal of outsider politics. This longer-range view will help us to see that the causes of the present populist moment lie further back than recent waves of immigration or the 2008 global financial crisis. They also have their origin in sociological changes to society that are making us question certain facets of democratic governance and pushing us to question how democracies are organised, and for whose benefit. I'll term this the *democratic grievance* approach to provide some symmetry with the other accounts we will consider.

Populism and economic grievance

If we are looking for the key reason why populism has erupted across the democratic world, and indeed across many less-developed countries, according to many commentators we need to think about the impact of the global financial crisis of 2008, which brought about recession and the response of many governments, austerity. Commentators in this camp include those who adopt a political economy approach, such as Mark Blyth (who has some excellent YouTube presentations on the topic), Colin Hay and Andrew Gamble. It's also the default setting for journalists in the financial press, who tend to locate major shifts in political life in terms of changes in the economy. How does the story go?

To recall the main events, up to 2006 the global economy enjoyed a significant period of growth that underpinned a boom in jobs, house prices and public finances. This led to the development of major infrastructure projects, expansion of public services and a more general sense of economic well-being that sustained the electoral success of moderate centre-left and centre-right politicians, such as Tony Blair, Bill Clinton, Gerhard Schröder and Nicolas Sarkozy, throughout the 1990s and early 2000s. This is not to say these people escaped criticism from either end of the political spectrum. For the left, this period was one of continuing hegemony of the market-based or neo-liberal policies that were the legacy of the previous generation of politicians, most notably Margaret Thatcher and Ronald Reagan. For the right, the concern was of open borders and the spreading of a multi-cultural mantra that the nation state was dead and that we had to embrace the free flow of peoples.

One of the features of the period was the steady deregulation of banks to promote, so it was argued, the greater liquidity needed to underpin investment. This was in the name of maintaining the boom conditions of the first decade of the twenty-first century.

Huge sums were invested in all kinds of 'vehicles' and 'derivatives', such as sub-prime mortgages in Latin America. Many banks became over-committed. What they owed others greatly outweighed the assets they could draw on if called on to repay their debts. In short, deregulation led to a financial bubble of unprecedented proportions.

As has now become part of popular folklore, and the subject matter of films such as *Inside Job* and *The Big Short*, the bubble burst in 2008. The Icelandic government, which had invested spectacular sums of money on the promise of massive returns, defaulted. It became clear that the issue was not confined to a relatively minor set of government-backed loans. Most of the major banks had seriously over-reached themselves. The structure wobbled, until Lehman Brothers went bust, leading to a meltdown of financial institutions on both sides of the Atlantic.

Faced with the prospect of a complete collapse of the banking sector and the wiping out of the savings of many millions of citizens, governments were left with little choice but to step in to cover the debts of the major banks and to provide enough liquidity from the public purse to keep the banking sector going. These measures succeeded in stabilising the situation but at major cost to public finances. Money that would have been spent on public services, infrastructure projects and investment in new companies and businesses was diverted to prop up the banks.

The immediate effect was a sharp downturn in the larger economy, producing a recession across the Western world. Factories closed. Orders for new products dried up. Investment in machinery and equipment dried to a trickle. Unemployment went up, spectacularly in countries heavily dependent on public investment, such as Spain and Italy.

Faced with a collapse in public finances, recession and a reduction in tax revenue, governments adopted austerity measures to cut back on expenditure. This translated into public wage freezes, reductions in the pensions of public sector employees and cutbacks in public health, education and housing budgets. A cruel wind blew through societies touched by financial crisis, leaving few unscathed. Needless to say, the bankers did just fine.

Unsurprisingly, citizens expressed their displeasure on the streets and at the ballot box. In Iceland, where the crash started, citizens took to the streets, in what became known as the 'Pots and Pans Revolution'. After protests at the national parliament, the citizens sacked their own government, charging a number of ministers with financial fraud and embezzlement. They then set up a constituent process to 'reboot' the political system with additional safeguards to promote financial transparency and ethical conduct. In Spain, millions of citizens took to town and city squares in a co-ordinated protest that became known as #15M after the day of action (15 May 2011) that marked the start of the protests. *Los Indignados* (the 'pissed off') promised to remain in occupation until the entire political class resigned.

This spectacle of citizens taking over their cities and indeed their political systems inspired perhaps the best-known response to the crisis, Occupy Wall Street. Occupy spread like wildfire, first across North America and then the rest of the world. Its slogan 'We are the 99%' expressed in direct terms people's disgust at the emerging polarity between a tiny elite that had enriched itself during the bad, as well as good times, and ordinary citizens left without savings or prospects.

This is just a snapshot of the mood in the months and years after the financial crisis. It left a bitter legacy of the public perception of the competence and probity of those in charge, the elites. Citizens were unmoved by whether the elites were centre-left or centre-right, or whether they wore a red or a blue tie. In the wake of crippling recession and austerity, fine distinctions between establishment politicians faded under an over-arching impression of incompetence and lack of humanity, evident in the failure to deliver basic welfare services. Unsurprisingly, citizens began to weary of mainstream parties and politicians, and in particular of centre-left or social democratic parties, which are usually expected to defend such services rather than impose austerity.

Retribution was swift. The UK prime minister, Gordon Brown, who mere months before the global financial crisis had crowed about the 'golden age' of finance at a dinner for bankers and financiers, was unceremoniously dumped from office in 2010. The President of France, Nicolas Sarkozy, languished ineffectually until 2012, when he was displaced by the equally ineffectual François Hollande, who would go on to receive the lowest-ever approval ratings for a French president, only surviving on the understanding that he would not stand again. Social democratic parties in Germany, Spain and Italy suffered along similar lines. They're still suffering as recent election results confirm.

The story repeated itself across the advanced democracies. Mainstream politics wilted under the onslaught of citizen disapproval and discontent. New parties and new figures, from outside or beyond the mainstream, began to gain traction with the electorate. Jeremy Corbyn, a quintessential outsider, well known for his far-left views and penchant for rebelling against his own party in Parliament was – to the astonishment of political commentators and indeed his supporters – elected leader of the UK Labour Party in 2015. Even more improbably, his election led to a massive influx of new members, to the point where Labour became the largest political party in western Europe, in terms of membership. Far from crashing in the 2017 general election, Corbyn ran the incumbent prime minister, Theresa May, close enough to give hope that the UK would shortly usher in its first-ever radical socialist government. His secret? A clear-eyed promise to abolish austerity.

Corbyn's rise took place against the backdrop of the Brexit referendum campaign in the latter half of 2015. How can we reconcile the rise of a far-left politician with a vote widely interpreted as a revolt against immigration and freedom of movement?

JEREMY CORBYN

Jeremy Corbyn is a long-standing Member of Parliament, and current leader of the British Labour Party. He is well known for his far-left political views, including support for the Irish Republican cause, the Palestinians and the regimes of Hugo Chávez in Venezuela and Fidel Castro in Cuba. He was a regular thorn in the side of Tony Blair's Labour administrations, voting against his own party more than 400 times when they were in government. With the resignation of Ed Miliband after the general election of 2015, he was persuaded to stand for the leadership, to give party members the choice of a left-wing candidate. Unexpectedly, he easily beat the three mainstream candidates. When his parliamentary Labour colleagues called for a vote of no confidence in him in 2016, he easily won that vote too. Labour increased its share of the vote in the 2017 general election, ensuring that Corbyn was able to cement his position during the vital period of Brexit negotiations.

It's a good question, and one that highlights the distinctiveness of the populism moment. Corbyn is no fan of the EU. Although his party campaigned on the Remain side, he was largely absent from the referendum campaign, much to the irritation of the political establishment and his party colleagues. While the question of immigration and the UK's control of its borders was important for some 'leave' voters, many others voted 'leave' as a gesture of disapproval of the political establishment and a rebuke to the political class after years of austerity. The Brexit vote was not binary, in this sense. And in the 2017 general election, many of those same voters backed Corbyn as a 'change' figure, who promised a fresh start.

Later in 2016, Trump triumphed in the American presidential election against the establishment candidate, Hillary Clinton. But it could easily have turned into a contest between two outsider figures, had Sanders won the Democratic nomination. Instead Trump was able to profit from people's discontent with the elites with his promise to 'Make America Great Again'. This sounded like an undertaking to restore America's military pre-eminence, but in the minds of the electorate it also pointed very firmly to a promise to restore economic pre-eminence against competition from China and East Asia. The undertaking to restore jobs lost to offshoring, to raise tariffs against imports, in the name of protecting American industry, to lower corporate taxes to promote economic growth and more generally to give hope to parts of America badly affected by recession was a major factor in his victory. His wins in the swing states of the Midwest and 'Rust Belt' America, including Pennsylvania, Wisconsin and Michigan were vital.

Even in this brief overview, it is difficult not to be impressed by the correlation between economic crisis and austerity on the one hand, and the recent rise of outsider figures and movements on the other. The global financial crisis certainly seems to have been a significant factor in generating citizen discontent with the established order, preparing the way for the rise of outsider figures promising a break from a now-humbled political establishment and its failed policies of neo-liberal globalisation and financialisaton that led to recession and austerity. The much-vaunted 'Third Way' between socialism and capitalism, which for two decades was the dominant socio-economic model underpinning the centre-right and centre-left axes, wobbled, leaving the way open for more radical figures who promised a real or imagined break from this model. In this economics-focused analysis, do we not have most if not all the components we need to explain the recent rise of populism?

Populism and cultural grievance

Few would deny that economic factors play a role in understanding the rise of populist movements and people such as Trump.

Hard times, recession and austerity make up a formula that might have been designed to stimulate discontent with the status quo. However, privileging economic factors leaves us wondering how to account for other parts of the populism story.

The result of the Brexit vote illustrates some of the limitations of the economic grievance case. Those who urged voting to remain in the European Union, which included senior members of both major parties, did so on the basis that leaving the EU would be harmful to the UK's economic prospects. This was backed up by detailed report after detailed report showing the impact of a 'leave' vote on the British economy. The Remain campaign, dubbed 'Project Fear' by Boris Johnson, among others, was designed to convince the electorate that they should vote with their heads and their wallets, not with their hearts and their Union Jacks. But 52% of those who voted were unmoved by these arguments, voting to leave and to sunder apparently vital links to the continent.

Beyond Brexit, we also must work out why many people in wealthy countries such as Holland, France, Austria and Germany have in increasing numbers turned their backs on the mainstream and adopted authoritarian populist figures and parties as their representatives. If the economic story is so compelling, surely citizens would continue supporting centre-left and centre-right parties that have delivered long-term economic stability, generous welfare provision and excellent prospects for young people? We might also mention the situation in the USA. If the global financial crisis were such a driver of political sentiment, why did it take so long for these sentiments to be expressed in presidential elections? It started in 2008, the year Barack Obama was elected president. Surely, if the electorate were keen to punish the incompetence of elites, he wouldn't have been re-elected in 2012? Even in 2016, the election was an undeniably close-run affair. Clinton, at one level a determinedly establishment figure, was beaten by the quirks of the electoral college system; she won the popular vote. If there is a correlation between economic performance and political outcomes, it is hardly linear and self-evident. There must be other factors to explain what's happening.

A compelling account that challenges the economic grievance thesis is provided by the journalist and author David Goodhart. In his provocative and much discussed work, *The Road to Somewhere*, he claims that populations in the advanced democracies have become divided between 'Anywheres' and 'Somewheres'. Anywheres are those who enjoy and benefit from the relatively open borders resulting from increased globalisation and co-operation between the advanced economies. They have a cosmopolitan outlook and do not see themselves as rooted to a particular location or a particular country. Rather, they see themselves as citizens of the world, enjoying different cuisines, different cultures and the ability to move around the globe as opportunities arise. Goodhart argues that Anywheres tend to assume everyone thinks like them. Much of the media, academia, the literati and the upper echelons of the political and economic classes are Anywheres. They dominate the airwaves, the op-ed columns, the lecture halls and policy institutes. They think globalisation equates to progress, that there is something for everyone in open borders and that in any case, since it cannot be reversed, one might as well 'go with the flow'. The reality, Goodhart says, is rather different.

Most people are Somewheres, not Anywheres. Somewheres typically live and work in the same place for most of their lives. Goodhart reports that 60% of the UK population will die within 25 miles of their birthplace, which starkly highlights the point. Somewheres do travel, but largely for holidays or for work, returning to their community after brief sojourns elsewhere. Their world is shaped by the people they grew up with and the people they work with. People who look like them and think like them; people with similar habits, values and beliefs. They are content with the familiar and do not crave life-altering experiences, such as moving to another continent. They like the world as it used to be, less so the world that is being created by the pressure of migration, globalisation and trans-nationalism. Whereas Anywheres see the influx of migrants as a welcome diversification of society, Somewheres see it as a threat to a way of life. The Somewhere sensibility dwells lovingly on a past that was simpler, easier to understand, more predictable and populated by people like them.

On this reading, Brexit and Trump represent the revolt of the Somewheres; what is otherwise called 'nativism'. When British citizens were asked whether they valued economic well-being over the maintenance of a certain cultural identity, the majority voted in favour of the latter. This wasn't a knee-jerk reaction. It wasn't an irrational impulse propelled by the fake promises of the Leave campaign. It was a desire, rightly or wrongly, to maintain a certain idea of what it means to be British. Anywheres assume that when the truth about the fate that awaits the British economy is fully apparent, the citizens will turn their back on Brexit and adopt the pragmatic internationalism of the Remain side. Their expectations are likely to be dashed. According to the British Attitudes Survey, the primary reason many voters chose 'leave' was to control immigration, restore British identity and repatriate powers lost to the EU back to Parliament. Economic factors were secondary; and sometimes not even that.

In the USA, Trump assumed an approach that put American interests front and centre, against the hand-wringing liberalism of Obama and Clinton, would appeal to the many Somewheres in the American heartlands who felt they had been ignored. Books such as *Hillbilly Elegy* by JD Vance explore this dynamic well. There's a huge hinterland in the USA that feels politics passes it by. Politicians jet to and from the east coast to the west coast, rarely stopping to engage with the folks in 'deep America', who lead lives far removed from the glitz and glamour of LA or New York as represented in the popular media. Trump well understood these sentiments, which is why he turned his back on the Anywheres in his own party in favour of an overtly nativist agenda of bringing jobs back to America, turning up the heat on China through increasing tariffs and ripping up years' worth of carefully-negotiated international agreements. This bonfire of internationalism was payback for the many Somewheres, who found in Trump someone who could articulate their frustrations and anger at decades of neglect.

The thesis of the power of cultural identity and the desire to retain the integrity of the nation is also useful in understanding the appeal of movements and parties on the European continent. Le Pen and the National Rally wrap themselves in the French flag while raising fears of a rising tide of Islamic demands in a country famous for its insistence on egalitarian and republican ideals. The influx of refugees and migrants from North Africa and the Middle East into Italy, Hungary, Austria and Germany accounts in large measure for the serious backlash suffered by mainstream parties in those countries and the rise of far-right parties promising to turn back the hordes and restore pride in nation and culture. On Goodhart's reading the rise of the far right could only be a surprise to those who have the outlook, the sensibility and the financial means to surf the opportunities presented by globalisation. For large swathes of the populations of advanced democracies the opportunities barely exist. Even if they did, many would turn their backs on them.

What about cultural grievance? Does this provide a more compelling account than those focusing on economic factors? Thinking about Goodhart's thesis, a number of issues need to be taken on board. Whether complex societies like the UK and USA can be neatly divided into two camps, even for illustration, is at least moot. His argument works well given the binary nature of the Brexit referendum and the American presidential election, not because there really are two neatly-divided camps. However, it has a useful symmetry: Somewheres voted 'leave' and Trump;

Anywheres voted 'remain' and Hillary. It's a nice, clean set of distinctions but that doesn't make it right.

The Brexit vote was quite a lot more complicated than these divisions suggest. The major cleavages in the electorate also included age; older voters were much more likely to vote 'leave' than those under the age of 24, who voted 72% in favour of 'remain'. Voters in Scotland and Northern Ireland chose 'remain', despite the fact that those regions no doubt have just as many Somewheres as the rest of the UK. Then there is the ideological dimension. Many left-wing Corbyn supporters, who might otherwise see themselves as Anywhere cosmopolitans, shared their leader's scepticism about the democratic credentials of the EU and voted 'Lexit' (Left Brexit). On the right, economic liberals such as Ken Clarke, a cabinet minister under Margaret Thatcher, and someone wedded to the notion that free trade requires open or at least porous borders, ignored the dominant Somewhere sensibility of their party membership to vote 'remain'.

The examples go on. Social class was a weaker predictor than age. The middle class was evenly split between Remain and Leave, whereas around 64% of skilled manual workers, as well as the working class and non-workers, voted to leave the EU. Given that the thrust of the Remain campaign was the anticipated impact of leaving on the British economy, it is clear both that the campaign backfired and that it left many of those predicted to be worse off unmoved. Issues around immigration and fear of the loss of identity seemed to have been more telling than economic considerations, certainly as far as less well-off sections of the electorate were concerned. This also appears to be the case across continental Europe. The rise of the far right is fed by economic insecurity, but economic factors do not themselves explain why citizens vote for Wilders, Le Pen, Orbán and Salvini. The perceived threat posed by the influx of refugees, mass migration and the Islamisation of Europe seem to be the more important drivers.

The rise of populism should not, however, be equated with the rise of far-right movements and parties, a mistake often made by media commentary looking for a dramatic angle on contemporary events. It is easy to overlook the fact that the populist insurgency of recent years also includes the rise of left-wing populisms, best represented by the emergence of *Podemos* in Spain and *Syriza* in Greece. The M5S, a big winner in the Italian general election of 2018, arguably has more in common with the left than the right, though its persistent Euroscepticism often means it is lumped together with right-wing movements and parties. How do matters look when we add consideration of left-wing populism into the mix?

Podemos and *Syriza* primarily gained traction with their electorates because of economic hardship caused by recession and the adoption of austerity measures to rein back public spending. *Podemos* self-consciously allies itself with the social movements and organisations that identify with #15M, which emerged from citizen discontent with the handling of the economic downturn, rather than any discontent with multiculturalism or immigration policies. On the contrary, forces identifying with #15M have repeatedly held demonstrations and actions in favour of open borders and help for refugees, regarding as inadequate the actions of the centre-right Spanish government to relieve the desperate plight of populations in North Africa and the Middle East.

Syriza came to power in Greece after a collapse in confidence in the government's handling of the debt crisis, which over several weeks and months in 2015 threatened to lead to 'Grexit'. Whilst Greece has witnessed the rise of resentment against refugees and migrants fleeing conflict, this has provided support for the far-right Golden Dawn party, not for *Syriza*, which remains firmly internationalist and European in outlook.

Left-wing populism adds another twist. Cultural factors, as defined in terms of identity, belonging and nationhood, play a relatively modest role, if they are not actually irrelevant to the

SYRIZA

Created in 2012, *Syriza* is a Greek political party, led by Alexis Tsipras, which began as a coalition of political parties from the left and far left of the Greek political spectrum. It took power in the elections of 2014. *Syriza*'s term in office has been notable for the almost-constant battle to stave off the country's bankruptcy through the renegotiation of loans to the 'Troika' – the International Monetary Fund (IMF), the European Commission and the European Central Bank (ECB). Yanis Varoufakis, who served as finance minister in 2015, argued that Greece should seek a renegotiation of these loans along more realistic lines, which would permit the reconstitution of the Greek economy on a sustainable basis. This proposal, which involved facing down the EU's finance ministers, was put to the Greek people in a referendum. Despite the 'yes' vote, Tsipras felt Greece had to follow the EU's line, leading to Varoufakis's resignation. Varoufakis went on to create his own movement (DiEM25 – Democracy in Europe Movement 2025), whose main objective is to democratise European institutions and increase their transparency and accountability, together with opening up its decision-making processes to greater participation by citizens and their representatives in a Constituent Assembly.

story. Instead, support for left populist parties comes largely from immediate economic factors, in particular from the dramatic rise in unemployment, the collapse of savings and pensions, wage freezes in the public sector and a lack of confidence in the competence of elites to manage macroeconomic issues.

Economic versus cultural grievance

The global financial crisis of 2008 is certainly a factor in the recent rise in support for both right-wing and left-wing populisms. On the right, economic crisis promotes the generation of a narrative in which the elites can be blamed for encouraging the outsourcing and offshoring of jobs to countries with lower labour costs and simultaneously encouraging the inflow of migrants to take low-paid jobs. Crisis shows the one-sided nature of globalisation: it enriches the owners of capital at the cost of the jobs of those left behind, particularly in former industrial and manufacturing heartlands such as 'Rust Belt' America, the north of England, north-eastern France and eastern Germany. On the left, the crisis shows the perils of financialisation and the dependency of poorer economies when tied to wealthier countries, as in the eurozone.

Right-wing populisms translate the resentment caused by economic crisis into 'cultural grievance' and a critique of the international order. On the right, economic crisis paves the way for 'nativist' movements and parties that promise a retreat from the international order and the promotion of national interests and national identity: 'Make America Great Again', '*Remettre La France en Ordre*' ('Sort France Out'), 'Britain: Forward Together'. On it goes. The problem is that countries have become entangled with bodies that do not prioritise the national interest: supranational organisations such as the European Union, the Trans-Pacific Partnership (TPP), the United Nations. The list is long. Nativism feeds on the instinct to look after our own affairs, to not be dependent on others, to reject the view that co-operation always leads to the best outcomes for the nation. Developing co-operation with 'friendly' states that share the same 'values' as us: yes. Engagement in complex international treaties that impose all manner of unwelcome obligations and duties: no.

Left-wing populisms translate into a critique of neo-liberalism and the idea that the market is always the best arbiter of individual and collective interests. Here, the immediate focus is on relieving the suffering of those hit hardest by recession and austerity: the unemployed, the young struggling to find work, families who lose their house because they cannot pay the mortgage, public sector workers forced to accept wage freezes and pension cuts. There is a call to increase the scope of state intervention, including the re-nationalisation of services or sectors privatised under previous regimes, and to tax the 'super profits' of banks and the wealthy who have benefitted from the sell-off of public services. It therefore seeks the restoration of the state as the guarantor of entitlement to health, housing and education. The left is also associated with a campaigning stance in relation to international bodies and treaties, which they see as serving the needs and interests of the market rather than citizens.

If we think in the round about what stimulated the emergence of populist leaders and parties in the run-up to the dramatic events of 2016, it seems clear we need to consider both economic and cultural factors. An over-emphasis on the economic will lead to downplaying the links, in right-wing narratives, between economic crisis and the need for a renewal of the nation. An over-emphasis on the cultural will lead us to downplay the way in which economic crisis produced the conditions for a critique of neo-liberalism and the adoption of the market as orthodoxy by the elites of both right and left over the previous forty years.

The populism puzzle

Have we assembled all the pieces needed to solve the puzzle of why populism has exploded across the advanced democracies? We can see that crisis has provoked a specific set of responses. We can see that citizens are fed up with how elites have tried to respond to this crisis. But there's an additional issue: citizens were fed up with elites *long before* the crisis of 2008, long before the recent waves of immigrants and refugees, long before austerity. What's the story?

Since the 1960s, there has been a noticeable, and much commented on, decline in peoples' engagement with mainstream electoral politics and democratic representation. Voter turnout has declined in nearly every advanced democracy, particularly at the supra-national level, such as European elections, and the sub-national levels of regional, local and municipal elections. The pattern is not uniform; not every country has suffered precipitous decline. But many have. Political scientists have scratched their heads for some time, trying to work out what's going on. But it's not just voting that causes concern.

Across the democratic world, political party membership is in free fall. Political parties are the key transmission belt between citizens and the system of governance, so the dramatic decline is of great concern to those interested in questions of democratic legitimacy. To take the UK as an example, in the 1960s around 30% of the electorate were members of a political party. Today that number is nearer two or three percent, though this has partially been offset by the impact of Jeremy Corbyn's leadership of the Labour Party, which has energised a constituency looking for a clear break with austerity policies. The problem does not stop there. Polling data suggest trust in politicians has been in decline for several decades, as has interest in electoral politics and the day-to-day business of legislatures, as measured by the column inches devoted to these matters in newspapers and the hours spent on television analysis.

In short, our emotional investment in democratic politics is declining, even if our belief that democracy is the best system of government largely remains robust. We are no longer deeply invested in a specific political party or ideology, and we understand political processes less well than earlier generations, who followed the detail of elections, parliaments, hearings and policy with much greater interest. In this context the emergence of radical figures, redemptive figures, heterodox movements and parties, and more generally outsider politics critical of existing elites, is hardly surprising.

All this predates the global financial crisis and the current populist 'moment': Jean-Marie Le Pen made it to the second round of the French presidential election in 2002; Pim Fortuyn, one of the first notable maverick anti-Islam European leaders, also made his breakthrough that year. Ralph Nader, Ross Perot and Rand Paul attracted considerable support in American presidential elections before the crisis hit. Pauline Hanson, of Australia's One Nation Party, came to prominence outside her home state, Queensland, in the late 1990s. Outsider parties and leaders have been a feature of politics for some time, and certainly from before the global financial crisis, highlighting the deficiencies of the elites and the need for a politics more attentive to the needs of the people.

Populism and 'democratic grievance'

The preparation of the ground for the emergence of populism has been happening for several decades. It has long preoccupied political scientists concerned about citizens' waning appetite for voting, and therefore the declining legitimacy of representative democracy. What lies behind this larger crisis of democratic participation and engagement? Why have citizens increasingly turned their backs on the mainstream, either by refusing to engage with the electoral process or by mandating leaders and parties who advertise themselves as outsiders?

One influential account frames the issue in terms of an emerging 'post-democracy'. This term was coined by the political scientist Colin Crouch, to express what he saw as the hollowing-out of democracy in the 1980s and 1990s, due to the embrace of neo-liberalism across the political spectrum. Governments of both the left and the right enacted what became known as 'New Public Management', a form of governance focused on the privatisation of public services, the import of private sector management techniques and the insistence on the use of market-based criteria to assess the worth or value of public goods.

With both left and right adopting a similar ideology, the vital sense of choice between the major political parties began to whither, to the point where citizens could no longer detect a significant difference. Choosing candidates at election time began to resemble choosing soap powder or kitchen cleaner: different wrappers for essentially the same product. This was reinforced by the emergence of what Richard Katz and Peter Mair term 'cartel parties' in place of parties with distinctive values, beliefs and ideologies. Parties became brands, rather than the repository of the needs, interests and ideals of particular social classes or particular parts of the population. They became disconnected and less likely to provide an engaging or involving experience for their members, more 'elite', as they huddled up to corporations for support.

This consensus of basic political orientation provided stability for democratic systems. Agreement across the political and economic elites translates into 'business as usual' politics, focused on problem-solving and generating solutions based on a shared analysis. So far so good. But the problem with such an approach is threefold: first, it generates a style of engagement that lacks drama, edge and a sense of something important being at stake. The similarity of candidates and programmes leads to somnolent politics: 'wake me up when it's over'. Second, it means that real contestation takes place outside or beyond the mainstream electoral process. Politics becomes something associated with social movements, with the street and with protests and demonstrations. Politics is elsewhere, not in parliament or congress. Third, it means that should a crisis affect confidence in the overall paradigm, it is easy for citizens to conclude that the elites are to blame and thus that solutions to the crisis need to come from outside or beyond that group.

In this view, the cause of the crisis that generated the populist insurgency is neo–liberalism. From the 1980s, the elites' adoption of virtually every advanced democracy of market-friendly policies made politics into a form of technocratic governance, rather than the contest of different visions, ideologies and world-views it seemed to have been in an earlier epoch. If it didn't quite kill off politics, neo-liberalism subordinated it to an agenda dictated from outside or beyond the nation state and thus the political community, leading to the impression that politics didn't matter. This was a matter for celebration for neo-liberals such as Margaret Thatcher, who famously declared that 'There is no alternative'.

Being told that there's nothing we can individually or col-lectively do to alter a state of affairs is a formula for turning us off politics. And that, for neo-liberals, was the point. Why encourage the thought that citizens can change their own social and eco-nomic arrangements when it was clear that the market held the answers to the fundamental question of how we should organise ourselves? Why argue that politics matters when it is economics and the market that should rule the roost? On this reading, it is not citizens who are 'anti-politics' but elites. It's elites that sought to persuade us that the state had become too inflated, too over-burdened, too much of an obstacle to the realisation of individual ends. The less state and politics we had, the freer we would be. So we were told.

The global financial crisis shook the neo-liberal paradigm to its core, paving the way for outsider figures who would save the people from economic catastrophe. This is not to say that all the outsiders agreed what needed to be done to clear up the mess. As we have heard, the right blamed globalisation, trans-nationalism and open markets for the misery. The left countered that the displacement of the state as the fulcrum of public life through privatisation and marketisation was to blame. A return to social democracy, or some sort of market-based socialism, was there-fore required to remedy the economic disaster. With the collapse of the neo-liberal paradigm it was hoped a properly democratic mode of governance would be restored.

Decadence and the decline of the political class

As well as focusing on the wider socio-economic context in which politics takes place, in recent decades political scientists have also tried to understand why the standing of politicians has declined, seemingly to the point of no return. Trust in politicians is at a low ebb. Recent studies have shown that we trust politicians even less than the professions that usually bear the brunt of our scepticism: second-hand car salesmen, lawyers and estate agents.

Part of this seems to be related to the changing function of the media over the past half-century. For most of the twentieth century, the function of the media in relation to politics was to report on matters of parliament, affairs of state and the principal dramas affecting the nation. The press kept a respectful distance from the private lives of public figures, fearing the wrath of a population brought up on the idea that those in office were there to serve the public interest and thus deserved respect.

Over the latter half of the twentieth century, the public developed a taste for tales of scandal and corruption. There was no shortage of titillating stories. In the UK, the Profumo affair of 1963 was a turning point. An unbeatable combination of spies, sex and secrets sold newspapers and whetted people's appetite for more. With the emergence of social media and 24/7 news coverage the propensity to chase stories of a salacious kind has grown unchecked. The obvious victims of this media hurly-burly are the politicians. Every groping hand, every item of over-expenditure, every indiscreet aside, is now the stuff of public interest.

The net effect of this constant fixation on the lives and infelicities of politicians is to diminish any sense of their special vocation as guardians of the public interest. Politicians are now just another kind of public figure seeking our attention. They've joined 'celebrity society', with the caveat that they are for the most part less entertaining, less engaging and less aware than musicians or film stars of what this means. Additionally, they now find themselves in competition with the latter for the hearts and minds of the public. Bob Geldof and Bono campaign on behalf of starving Africans. Brigitte Bardot and Naomi Campbell campaign on behalf of animals. Elton John fundraises for AIDS charities. Whatever gap there was between politicians and celebrities is narrowing, with Donald Trump's election the crowning moment in the process of erosion.

Why does this matter? The credibility of democracy relies in large measure on the belief that our representatives, the politicians, are representing *us* rather than *themselves*. We need to feel that they care about our needs and interests, that they are in it for the public good, not for their own gain. But we have become less convinced that this is the case. Drip by drip, media coverage erodes our confidence in our representatives. Constant tales of scandal, corruption, patronage, nepotism and self-serving behaviour makes it easier for us to think of politicians less in terms of *who* they are and more in terms of *what* they are: '*la casta*', 'the elites', 'Washington', 'the pollies', 'them'.

The decline of the standing of representatives, combined with our propensity to see politicians as an undifferentiated self-serving group opens the way for a politics built on the qualities of individuals who are like 'us' rather than like 'them'. In place of identikit toothy politicians with over-rehearsed answers, the new conjuncture calls for 'authenticity'. Outsider politicians such as Bernie Sanders and Jeremy Corbyn clearly evince these qualities of authenticity. Both back causes mainstream figures believe have been lost long ago. They speak with conviction and believe that the world can be changed if only we tried hard enough. They refuse to kowtow to their parties' version of 'reality'. In short, they are principled idealists who can offer a vision of sunny uplands without reproach. Even those who don't agree with their beliefs respect their honesty, their approachability and the fact that they have held more or less the same views for half a century. They say what they think, not what the party *apparatchiks* have told them to say.

Further afield, a similar dynamic underpinned the unexpected victories of Ada Colau and Manuela Carmena, who won the 2015 municipal elections in Barcelona and Madrid respectively. Neither is a professional politician. Both were reluctant candidates who had to be persuaded by activists to stand, on the basis that they best represented the values and sentiments of the citizen platforms thrown together after #15M. Both are plain-speaking 'anti-political politicians', anti-political in the sense that they stand against what politics had become in Spain: over-professional, patronage-based, corrupt and indifferent to the needs and interests of the less well-off. The success of the Five Star Movement in the Italian general election of 2018 owes much to

FIVE STAR MOVEMENT

The Five Star Movement (M5S) was created in 2009 by Beppe Grillo, a comedian, activist and frequent media commentator. Grillo is well known in Italy for his critique of the political class and the state of Italian and EU politics, which he characterises as corrupt, inefficient and nepotistic. Grillo has long advocated using the Internet to do away with the representative elements of democratic governance in favour of a direct mandate from citizens. The party was created using Meetup, a social networking website, to generate a support base and M5S still sees itself as a virtual rather than traditional political entity. The five stars in its name refer to the five key elements of its programme: public water, sustainable development, the right to Internet access, sustainable transport and environmentalism. Grillo has never stood as a candidate but remains a mentor and father figure to the movement. In 2016, M5S enjoyed success in the municipal elections, securing victories in Rome and Turin. After a further breakthrough in 2018, when it secured the largest number of votes in the general election, M5S joined the governing coalition with *Lega*.

this phenomenon as well. Created by Beppe Grillo, a comedian who delights in taking potshots at the elites, the very rationale for M5S is 'anti-political'. It is self-consciously constructed as a protest party, a party for the alienated and disenchanted.

It is but a step from the authentic, anti-political politician to populism, which, as we noted in the last chapter, is seen as rotating around the special characteristics of the leader. Unlikely though it may seem, authenticity and honesty have emerged in this respect as special characteristics. Why? Because they stand in stark contrast to the over-spun quality of today's identikit politicians.

The rise of the citizen consumer

Political scientists tend to focus on the supply side of the political equation: what policies politicians and political parties offer to engage the public. The demand side, the needs and perspectives of citizens, is less commented on. Citizens used to be enthusiastic participants in the democratic process. Now we are much less so. What happened? Dominant accounts touch on two processes that can easily be confused: 'individualisation' on the one hand and 'individualism' on the other.

Individualisation is linked to modernisation theory and the view that one of the characteristics of modernity is the progressive erosion of group and collective identity and its replacement with self-chosen, uncertain and hybrid identities. This reflects a view of modernity marked by an intensification of migration, the collapse of feudalism and new modes of production that make it progressively harder to place people in a social class. This matters, because political parties were set up in the nineteenth century to represent particular identities, interests and ideologies. Social democratic parties were set up to represent the working class, Conservative and Liberal parties to represent the middle class, Catholic parties to represent Catholics, and so on. With the progressive erosion of these identities, we feel less affinity with the parties and organisations whose rationale it is to defend us. We come to think of ourselves less in terms of the categories of identity ascribed to us (white, British, working class, etc.) and more in terms of the needs, interests and desires we develop as distinct people.

Individualism, by contrast, refers to a moral, ethical and ultimately political stance that favours the needs and interests of individual people over those of classes or social groups. In the hierarchy of core political values, it favours individual liberty over social equality. In sociological terms individualism is also linked to the view that politics is ultimately about choices. Liberty means having choices and exercising them, whether as citizens or as consumers: politics resembles the supermarket. Political parties develop brands that represent particular kinds of social good. At election time we choose the brand we have an affinity for and want to see succeed.

The individualisation thesis has been influential in explaining why political participation is changing character. As political sociologists note, we might be less inclined to join political parties, but it doesn't mean that we have given up on politics. Politics now means getting involved in campaigns against injustice, writing blogs, taking part in protests, connecting with others for purposes or causes. This kind of informal, street or 'subterranean' politics has exploded over the past few decades as it has become easier for citizens to find each other without the need to join a political party or subscriber-based organisation.

The net effect of these developments is to reinforce the image of politics as taking place elsewhere, without the need for intermediaries, politicians and representatives. It has further fed the idea that democracy should not be about mandating someone to represent us but rather to act and participate ourselves, without the need for politicians. In this view, representative democracy comes to resemble a power grab by the well off. What should be the concern of all citizens has been kidnapped by elites, who as a result exercise a de facto monopoly over our lives. This was the mood generated in the Occupy protests, and those in Iceland and Spain. In Spain, the slogan *Democracia Real Ya*, which became a motif of the protests, sums the matter up. 'Real Democracy Now!' meaning democracy of and by the people, as opposed to the elites, a democracy based on citizens' participation and direct engagement in the political process, not on the monopolisation of power by *la casta*, or the 1%.

For all the clamour of new social movements and emergent forms of 'connective action', the individualism thesis gives us a different perspective for understanding how citizens behave in the advanced democracies. It starts from the observation that most citizens are becoming increasingly less politically active. Many of us don't join organisations, either virtual or real. Indeed, many of us don't vote or get involved in politics of any kind. We seem to be apathetic and self-absorbed by our daily lives. At best we have become 'clicktivists' or 'slacktivists', conflating the momentary effort required to register our disapproval with an angry face emoticon with real mobilisation. When we do get involved it is less with a view to improving the lot of the collective than with maximising benefits for ourselves or our pet concerns: endangered species, sweatshops in the developing world, floating plastic in the oceans. We have developed a distinctly consumerist mindset when it comes to politics, reflected paradoxically in our anticonsumerist insistence that we can change the world through the choices we make in the supermarket, or rather organic food shop. This is fed by an ideology that places choice at the heart of its claims about what we desire as citizens.

Matthew Flinders, author of *Defending Politics*, which seeks to understand the processes at work in our rejection of mainstream parties and politicians, picks up on this in his account of where democracy is failing. He argues that the consumerist mindset has led us to develop an unrealistic set of expectations for assessing politicians' performance. We want more and better public services, but we also want to pay less tax. This sets up a classic 'management of expectations' problem, with the difficulty that it is not the politicians who set the expectations but the media, public commentary and citizens. We project values and standards on to politicians that we ourselves would never be able to meet. We complain, for example, about the high pay of our representatives, barely acknowledging that many professionals would turn their nose up at a similar salary.

In short, we have set up democratic politics to fail, by setting expectations only a super-human with an uncontaminated record of public service could meet. We know where this is heading. A heady concoction of bile directed at over-paid and under-performing 'elites' and undue faith in an 'outsider' promising a fresh start or a return to a, much better, imagined past.

Space precludes an assessment of the strengths and weaknesses of the different approaches to understanding the nature of the crisis that democracy finds itself in. Some theories resonate strongly in certain kinds of democracy or in certain parts of the world, whereas others seem more applicable elsewhere. However, what seems less contentious is the notion that representative democracy finds itself undergoing a significant transformation across the globe. This is leading to the development of demands on democracy that seem to be difficult, if not impossible, to meet in the existing party-based paradigm.

This does not add up to a consistent critique of democratic governance. It's not that those who are disappointed or angered by democracy agree on what needs to happen for it to function better. Rather, we have a jumble of contradictory demands, reflecting a variety of political preferences. On the right, there is a desire for 'strong leadership', the reassertion of authority, low taxes and a redefinition of citizenship towards a specific kind of national identity. On the left, there is a desire for more inclusive

THE CRISIS OF DEMOCRACY

The idea that democracy is in crisis is held by many political scientists, politicians and commentators. Indeed, some suggest that if it has not actually died (as per the title of John Keane's book *The Life and Death of Democracy*), it has transmuted into 'post-democracy', 'kleptocracy' (governance by theft) or some other variant of 'plutocracy' (government of the rich). This is a response to the downturn, since the 1960s, of many of the leading indicators used to measure the health of democracy: voter turnout, membership of political parties, trust in politicians and interest in politics, as determined by how much we read about politics or watch politics-related content on television. There are also concerns about the erosion of 'electoral integrity' – the degree to which elections can be said to be 'free and fair'. However, not all specialists are convinced that democracy is in crisis, or that there is something new and particularly serious about the current state of affairs. David Runciman notes in *The Confidence Trap* that educated opinion has held liberal democracy to be in crisis since the late nineteenth century. He also comments that there are periods when the perception of crisis has been much more marked than at present, notably the 1930s. Others point to the evidence of regular large-scale surveys, such as the Eurobarometer, noting the persistent support for democratic institutions even among those with little inclination to vote or mandate politicians. Even where commentators agree there is a crisis, there is little consensus on the nature of the underlying causes or what is to be done.

or participatory styles of democratic governance, to promote engagement by the people ('the 99%'), as opposed to a corrupt or inefficient elite, and a critique of the penetration of society and the public sphere by narrow market criteria.

Both sets of democratic grievances can by styled 'populist'. Both lay the blame at the feet of elites, albeit for different reasons. Both see the solution in terms of entrusting the people to decide or determine for themselves how they wish to be governed, and indeed whether they wish to be governed at all. Both are convinced that new and 'authentic' leadership is required to bring about a transformation in democratic life.

Conclusion

Both economic and cultural forms of explanation are needed to understand what's going on around us. However, each points to the emergence of a different kind of populism. Cultural grievance tends to lie at the root of right-wing and far-right forms of populism. Economic grievance is more obviously at the root of left-wing populisms and the critique of neo-liberalism. Recession and austerity undoubtedly catalyse the development of resentment against migrants and refugees 'stealing jobs', and thus by extension cultural grievance. If we add a third dimension, democratic grievance, then we get a sense of the longer-term trends and tendencies that might otherwise be left out of the picture. This is needed to frame populism as a response not only to economic crisis and the impact of globalisation, but also to the hollowing out of representative politics that has been occurring for the past half-century or so. In the void created by a collapse in confidence in mainstream centrist parties, outsider politics has flourished, and will continue to flourish if these trends and tendencies are not addressed.

But we need to be careful before rushing to summarise how this process is preparing the ground for populism. The decline of democracy does not have a single cause, but rather reflects a series of sociological changes in society that are feeding into new kinds of demand and new kinds of representative claim, some of which cannot be met in our existing way of organising ourselves. Populism is less the cause of democratic decline, as is sometimes implied in the media, so much as an effect or a symptom of a wider crisis. But it is very much in populism's interest to maintain, and indeed build on, the perception that things are going wrong and that normal politics, mainstream parties and regular politicians cannot cope and need to be replaced by those who can. Populism is a product of crisis, but it also needs crisis to maintain its momentum, efficacy and appeal. 'Normality', however defined, is the enemy of populism. Is this to say that populism necessarily represents a threat to democracy? Or paradoxically, do we *need* populism for it to be renewed?

4

Is populism a threat to democracy?

To ask if populism is a threat to democracy will no doubt strike some as a curious question. Populism is, as far as many people are concerned, about political extremes, about red-cheeked demagogues hurling abuse at opponents while craving adoration from their supporters. From this point of view, populism seems to have much in common with authoritarianism and fascism: they are showy, boisterous styles of politics, in marked contrast to the sober, sensible affairs associated with functional democracies. How could populism, which looks and sounds very different to democracy, not be a threat to it?

Surprising as it may at first seem, this is a contentious issue. People are not querying whether it is good or bad to see incivility and intolerance creep into politics. The issue is whether the emergence of a more aggressive style of politics has much to do with populism, or whether it has resulted from the values and beliefs of those who might be using a populist strategy to advance their goals. Populism is used not only to describe far-right, 'nativist' movements, but also leftist movements that do not generally share the former's negative stance on minorities, Islam or refugees, to take three victim groups that regularly attract the ire of the right.

Populism and the threat to democracy

Trump's verbal assaults on Hillary Clinton ('Lock Her Up!'), Nigel Farage's intemperate attacks on the EU and its officials (on EU President Herman Van Rompuy: 'You have the charisma of a damp rag and the appearance of a low-grade bank clerk'), Marine Le Pen metaphorically draping herself in the French flag like a latter-day Marianne, Wilders' criticism of Islam ('I don't hate Muslims,' he once explained to the *Observer*. 'I hate their book and their ideology.'). None of this looks or feels like democracy, certainly as far as the classic portraits are concerned. Democracy should be even-handed, sensible and public-spirited. It should be about individual people doing the best they can for their society: 'Ask not what your country can do for you, ask what you can do for your country,' as President JF Kennedy memorably intoned.

To get at the root of the relationship between populism and democracy we need to move beneath the surface of media portrayals and clichés to evaluate the arguments of those who are convinced there is something there beyond bluster or rudeness. What, in short, makes populism a threat, as opposed to just a noisy, obnoxious style of politics, which we might object to more on aesthetic grounds than anything substantive?

Pluralism versus monism

If there is one argument that unites critics of populism, it is the defence of pluralism, the idea that in any complex society there will be all sorts of views about how we should live, different religions, different worldviews, and different ways of thinking about freedom, equality and justice. It's an argument that pops up in recent books by, among others, Jan-Werner Müller (*What is Populism?*), William Galston (*Anti-Pluralism: The Populist Threat to Liberal Democracy*) and Yascha Mounk (*The People vs Democracy*).

Populism's claim is that the people need to reclaim power and sovereignty from the elites. Think of the kind of claims advanced by Trump, Farage and Le Pen. Trump rails against 'Washington', accusing elites of having neglected working Americans in pursuit of their own interests. Farage accuses the British establishment of being in cahoots with the EU, leaving the people powerless in the face of overwhelming bureaucracy. Le Pen accuses elites of being out of touch with the sentiments of citizens confronted with a tide of Muslim immigrants that is steadily diluting the sense of France as a Christian and European nation. 'Financial globalisation and Islamist globalisation are helping each other out,' she told her supporters as she launched her presidential campaign in February 2017. 'Those two ideologies aim to bring France to its knees.' This is classic populist rhetoric. But why is it undemocratic?

In its contemporary guise, democracy is about the management of differences among people. More specifically, it is about how we manage differences of opinion, viewpoint and ideologies in complex modern settings. Should more money be spent on public services or should we ensure, in the name of personal liberty, that people get to keep more of their own income? Does everyone have a right to free healthcare, or should access to healthcare be determined by income or inherited wealth? Should higher education, as a 'public good', be free or is it fairer that we pay for something that benefits us rather than society?

Much of this boils down to a difference of values. Liberals tend to favour the needs and interests of the individual over the collective. Socialists, and those on the left, tend to prioritise welfare spending and public services over the right of an individual person to enjoy benefits that others cannot. This is reflected in our system of government, through the election of political parties' representatives, who are then held accountable by the electorate on how they put these values into practice. If more people favour free higher education than university fees, this will be reflected in their preferences at the ballot box and eventually in national policy. Modern democracy is 'majoritarian'; what is decided depends on where majority opinion lands. More or less. There's always a debate in political science about how well electoral systems reflect the will of the majority. But the point is that we're used to the idea that the 'will of the people' is interchangeable with 'the will of the majority of the people who voted or took part in a referendum'.

The concern with populists is that they don't seek to disentangle individual opinions from that of 'the people'. They don't recognise differences of viewpoint, ideology or personal preference as being fundamental to understanding how society should work. Instead they believe that government should be based on the views and needs of 'the people', considered as a distinct entity. No further distinctions are regarded as being significant or – and here's the point – legitimate or worth listening to. Another way of putting it is that populism is at odds with liberalism. It doesn't see individual liberty, views and opinions as primary values. It wants the 'Will of the People' to prevail. Too bad if your personal view doesn't happen to coincide with it.

To critics of populism, this destroys the understanding at the heart of democratic governance: that democracy has to be *liberal* democracy. Some critics detect the dark hand of the eighteenth-century political philosopher Jean-Jacques Rousseau here, with his influential idea that society should be governed by the 'general will', which is to say laws and rules to which everyone should consent. It's a neat illustration of the distinction commentators want to make between the populist and the pluralist conceptions of democracy. Pluralists insist that under democratic conditions all we can establish is what everyone, individually, chooses: 52% of UK voters want Brexit and 48% do not. Rousseau felt that governing a society on such a 'majoritarian' basis was unsatisfactory.

We should aim for a society that unites the people, that creates consensus, rather than aggregating votes or preferences to arrive at 'the will of all'. Wouldn't it be better to govern on the basis of laws and policies that are in everyone's interests, the 'general will'?

This sounds attractive but the problem has always been to establish what is in everyone's interests without ending up with a majority view. Rousseau himself was rather vague on the matter, leaving it open to a variety of interpretations. The suspicion has long been that the 'general will' would quickly collapse into 'the will of the leader or party who understands what the people want'. This is the problem with the populist account of representation. It proposes a shortcut between the people and a leader who intuitively knows what we want. As Müller nicely puts it, '[t]he leader correctly discerns what we correctly think and sometimes he might just think the correct thing a little bit before we do'.

Populism is thus undemocratic, because it refuses to acknowledge that different opinions, philosophies or ideologies have any weight or value. In positing the idea of the people as a homogenous entity with no differences in needs and interests, it dissolves the understandings that fed through into the development of democracy as a plural system of governance in which political parties and other actors articulate different viewpoints, policies and priorities. Populism threatens this, because it says we need a government based on the general will, not one based on the will of all. It appears to be a hyperextension of democracy but this is an illusion. Ultimately what 'the people' want or need is a cipher for what the leader and his or her coterie want or need. Agree or get out of the way. Mudde and Kaltwasser put this ambivalence clearly:

> ... *populism is essentially democratic but at odds with liberal democracy, the dominant model in the contemporary world. Populism holds that nothing should constrain 'the will of the (pure) people' and fundamentally rejects the notions of pluralism and therefore minority rights as well as the 'institutional guarantees' that should protect them.*

Redemption versus problem-solving

Populism is a redemptive style of politics. The point is not to make government run better, to provide improved public services or to resolve the very many puzzles that legislators manage day-to-day. It is the promise of a better country, a better world, a happier and more contented people. Marine Le Pen promises to make France more secure, more united and more 'French'. Beppe Grillo promises an end to the corrupt, client-and-patron form of governance that has held Italy back for decades. Bernie Sanders offers 'a future to believe in'. Jeremy Corbyn promises a government 'for the many and not the few'. Populism is long on promise and short on detail. It offers a rosy future without telling us how it will be achieved, or what resources it will need.

While the vagueness and generality of the promise is one of populism's chief strengths as a campaigning and mobilising style of politics, once in power it may become a source of disappointment that leads to citizens' disillusionment. Populism trades on high expectations. It's what makes it such an emotionally engaging and attractive political force. Populists don't have to temper their message to limited budgets or the difficulties of improving citizens' lives. This very optimism, combined with an extravagant view of its efficacy, creates the dynamic associated with populist regimes: an intolerance of independent institutions, such as the free press, the judiciary and the civil service.

In a democracy, independent institutions provide a counterweight to the government's message. They draw our attention to policies that are failing, people who are not complying, visions that are not being realised. They provide a safeguard against the abuse of power. Knowing this, populists are inclined to get on the front foot early to undermine confidence in and support for such institutions. Think about Trump's approach to managing the press corps; the startling way he accused some of the most respected American media outlets of peddling fake news, negative stories and narratives of failure, before declaring them 'enemies of the people'. In the UK, pro-Brexit campaigners have been at more-or-less constant war with the media about news relating to the impact of Brexit on the economy. Understanding the importance of predicted economic indicators for people to judge whether to support Brexit, campaigners constantly rail against those sections of the media inclined to a sceptical view of the likely impact of departure from the EU.

Brexit campaigners also threaten the judiciary and the civil service. When the Supreme Court upheld an application to ensure that the UK Parliament would be given a vote on whether to press on with the result of the referendum, they were accused of being 'traitors' by elements in the media close to the Brexit campaign. When the civil service published its report on the likely impact of Brexit on British exports, forecasting negative effects, it was accused of bias and disloyalty. A common theme in contemporary populist discourse is an assault on experts and expertise, the code for someone who doesn't agree with a particular policy or a particular stance.

The populist instinct is to manipulate, suppress, cajole and intimidate independent institutions and civil society into compliance with its worldview. This is contrary to the nature and form of democratic governance, which is built on a respect for, and acknowledgement of, the independence of institutions. These bodies keep politicians honest, serve the public interest by ensuring accountability and transparency and alert us to the abuse of power. Undermine them or worse, eliminate them, and we are naked before state power and but a short step from authoritarianism and fascism.

Modernity versus feudalism

Populism is about leaders and leadership. The leader possesses the message of redemption. The leader's charisma attracts supporters and mobilises them behind the message. Populists have occasionally set up their own party, as did Beppe Grillo and Pim Fortuyn. But they can also take over existing ones and make them their own. Trump found a party in a state of trauma after two election defeats, willing, in a pragmatic Faustian bargain, to sacrifice its soul to be elected. The Le Pens didn't exactly create the FN so much as create a strong brand association. Jeremy Corbyn didn't need to create a party but he did need to make it his own, signing up hundreds of thousands of new members and mobilising his support group ('Momentum') inside the party, making it almost impossible for anyone to remove him. From being an outsider in his own party, he became the outsider's outsider by signing every social ill to his own cause.

For critics the emphasis on the leader represents a return to a pre-modern or feudal arrangement. Under feudalism, everyone owed their position and their privileges to the monarch. Loyalty to the leader was the tie that bound them. Feudalism was progressively displaced by processes that made the governors accountable to the governed, replacing relationships built on personal and family connections with ones built on the functional qualities of office. Monarchs were replaced by presidents, duly elected by those qualified to vote. Ministers and office-holders became accountable to parliaments and legislatures, themselves composed of elected representatives. Personal rule fell, in favour of institutions and processes designed to guarantee accountability, stability and transparency of government.

Populism cuts against the grain of what democracy has come to mean, how it functions and on what basis. With so much emphasis on the omniscience and far-sighted properties of the leader, it tends to develop into a personality cult, which puts other institutions under strain. Criticism of the leader becomes criticism of the regime and, implicitly, a threat to the political order. There is no better illustration than Trump's court. The constant firing and hiring, coming and going of officials, advisers and confidants is deeply reminiscent of feudalism. It is also reminiscent of earlier authoritarian and fascist regimes, in which leaders regularly purged their immediate ranks to safeguard their position and undermine the possibility of rivals emerging.

Populism studies literature has long documented this dynamic in the developing world, and particularly in Latin America. Political instability leads to social breakdown, which leads to the demand for a strong leader or *caudillo* to clear up the mess. The leader develops a patronage-based regime, which sees the advantages of vesting in the leader an air of supernormal powers, to guarantee their power base and by extension the privileged position of those they support. Such has often been the pattern over the past century or so; it resurfaced in the Brazilian elections of 2018 with the election of Jair Bolsonaro, a former officer in the military. Bolsonaro's success owes much to his promise of a fresh start after a period when the probity of the political class was called into question. A quintessential *caudillo*, he is a strict disciplinarian who promises to restore law and order. He revels in his media image as an uncompromising figure, ready to take on the marginal elements of Brazilian society: the migrants, the street poor and the LGBT community. Bolsonaro was quoted in the *Guardian* as saying 'Brazilian society doesn't like homosexuals' and in the *New York Times*, responding to migrants arriving, as saying, 'the scum of the world is arriving in Brazil, as if we didn't have enough problems to resolve'. His power base relies, in classic fashion, on family and a wide network of dependants rallying to the cause: 'Brazil above everything; God above everyone.'

We have fewer examples to call on in the older democracies, and those we do have are not encouraging. In Hungary, Viktor Orbán took over an ex-communist but fully-democratic regime, with a sophisticated civil society, free press and media, all under the watchful eye of the European Union. None of this prevented him from emasculating much of civil society, generating a bitter and divisive discourse and putting in place a regime that much more closely resembles one-party authoritarianism than the democracy it displaced. Bloomberg reported election monitors as remarking on the 'shrinking space for informed political debate' in the Hungarian election of 2018, noting controls on media reporting and Orbán's rhetoric, which rotated around a rejection of liberalism and pluralism. In short, populism's fascination with charismatic leadership has negative consequences for democracy, in which leaders are expected to be accountable, either directly to the electorate or to legislatures. The institutions are supposed to be primary under democratic conditions, not the leader.

The claim against populism is compelling. Left unchecked, it corrodes the key attributes of democracy. These attributes include a respect for, and acknowledgement of, important differences as far as individual values and beliefs are concerned, recognition of civil society as an autonomous sphere with the licence to criticise the state as and when citizens decide and prioritisation of institutions and processes over personal qualities, charisma and the capricious qualities of individual leaders. Democracy is above all a system of governance involving checks and balances, a free press and independent institutions such as

VIKTOR ORBÁN

Viktor Orbán is the leader of the *Fidesz* party in Hungary. He has been elected as prime minister three times, most recently in 2018. He is noted for his far-right political views and for adopting a stance of democratic 'illiberalism' in response to the perceived threat posed by an influx of refugees from southern Europe and the Middle East. He is also noted for his Euroscepticism, frequently criticising the European Union for its weakness in defending the continent against mass migration. He has been accused of undermining democracy in Hungary by a series of reforms designed to water down the independence of institutions such as the judiciary and the free press. More generally, his politics is noted for being conservative, nationalist and pro-free-market.

the judiciary and a non-partisan public service to serve the government, not be its plaything. Anything that threatens either part of that system, or the whole system, represents a threat to democracy. That includes populism.

Populism and democratic renewal

It's not difficult to recognise this account in the many media reports and analyses of the current populist insurgency and what it represents for democracy. There are differences of nuance and emphasis, but by and large the consensus is that populism is bad for democracy and should be appropriately opposed and resisted. However, this isn't the whole story. We will continue to discuss what the concept means, and therefore whether we're really discussing the same phenomenon or confusing populism with authoritarianism, fascism or any kind of politics that seeks to bully a minority.

Others are more ambivalent about populism, conceding that there may well be democratic content in the chief claim; that the people should be the subject of politics. However, they remain fearful about how such an insight can be put into practice without risking essential features of democratic governance, such as an independent judiciary and competitive elections. Some commentators concede that under certain conditions populism *might* have a role to play in mobilising citizens behind a project to renew society, for example in parts of the developing world where, without a strong unifying leadership, social disintegration may await.

There is some suggestion in the literature that there may be a place for populism but this is usually framed in terms of *exceptions*, as opposed to a bridge to thinking about the utility of populism for democracy. Perhaps populism might be justified under certain conditions. Some, for example, have suggested that where strong leadership is needed to initiate or maintain the process of institution-building, we might need to make allowances. We could perhaps think of populism as a prelude to democracy, or as part of a process of democratisation, just so long as it is kept a long way away from our democracy, the democracy of the advanced industrial states. Then, there is less ambivalence. Populism is a menace and – as far as most writers on the topic are concerned – should be opposed.

There is, however, at least one school of political analysis that has consistently defied the tide. This school is associated with the work and legacy of the Argentinian political theorist Ernesto Laclau, author of a major work on the topic, *On Populist Reason*. For Laclau, populism is not only compatible with the operation of democracy, it is the best strategy for *renewing* and expanding democracy. He and Chantal Mouffe, his co-author on many key works, call this 'radical democracy'. In their view, we should put our fears of populism to one side, embrace populism and see its potential to generate forms of politics to fully engage people whose needs and interests are often overlooked. The renewal of democracy must be conceived of as a project, as well as a process. And as a project it needs to appeal to those who are the subject of democracy, the people themselves.

This is a very different reading of the nature, form and potential of populism. Many of the understandings that underpinned the mainstream's hostility to populism are implicitly – and often explicitly – queried by Laclau. This has inspired a distinctive account of populism that contrasts strongly with the dominant populism studies approach and that of many contemporary journalists. Laclau's work continues to inform analysis amongst progressive political theorists, sometimes called the 'Essex School' after the university in which he was a professor for many years. It is also widely discussed amongst activists on the left. The founders of *Podemos*, the Spanish party set up after #15M, happily acknowledge his influence and indeed embrace the term populism in the manner he encouraged.

Laclau's account of populism is certainly distinctive. It's also rendered in a demanding technical language that asks a lot of non-experts. On the other hand, his work has been so influential both in scholarly debates about populism and among activist circles that it is well worth persevering with.

Politics as the struggle for 'hegemony'

In Laclau's view, there is nothing unusual about a politics that appeals to 'the people'. Or rather, in a *democracy* there is nothing unusual about appealing to the people. Under democratic conditions the people, the *demos*, are the subject of democracy. Politicians appeal to the people all the time, though we might hear them use other terms: they might talk about 'ordinary working people' or 'the battlers' (a favoured term in Australia). They might talk about 'the vast majority' or 'sensible men and women'. This amounts to the same: an appeal to the people as they seek the broadest possible approval for their vision of how society should work, how we should organise ourselves, who should get what. We rarely hear politicians appeal directly to the sectional interests that might be their constituency. They don't often say 'this policy is good for the middle class but not the rest of you'; they say 'we need to help business because this is good for the country'. When Trump cut corporation taxes he didn't say, 'I'm doing this to make wealthy people richer.' He said policies like these are needed to make the whole country better off. He translated a policy that appealed strongly to part of his supporter base into a policy that allegedly helps everyone, the people. Nothing new in this, which is Laclau's point. Translating policies that improve the condition of one part of society into policies that sound like they will benefit everyone is key to maintaining electoral support.

For Laclau, there is nothing inherently undemocratic in this. Far from it. A campaign that doesn't seek to reach beyond narrow, sectional or particular interests is doomed to remain on the margins; the province of 'protest' or 'special interests'. If we want our vision of society, our values and beliefs, to gain traction, we need the people on our side. This, in a nutshell, is what seeking 'hegemony' means. It describes a situation in which the dominant worldview, and those who are identified with it, enjoy wide support. It indicates that citizens fully consent to the social order, which as a consequence does not need overt force or violence to maintain itself. Under democratic conditions, all political parties and projects seek hegemony. They seek to convince as many people as possible that they should support, vote for, be excited by and otherwise see as desirable their vision of how society should look.

So far, so good. The question then becomes that of how to get people to support your view. You need leadership. Someone must articulate the vision. Having a charismatic person who can do that is the best means of reaching the broadest number of people. Slogans, values and ideals do not sell themselves; they must be sold by someone. This is why leadership is so important, and why the question of who leads a given party or movement is of vital interest to party members and the voting public. The leader 'condenses' the message, embodies it and makes it real for citizens.

Success in politics usually depends on having someone who can articulate the core message of the broader movement or party in clear, compelling and convincing terms. Leaders need charisma, but they do not all have to look the same, sound the same or all be domineering extroverts. There are different styles and ways of articulating messages. But leaders do need to be effective communicators, able to reach beyond a party's natural constituency to appeal to the broader electorate. This is how politics works in contemporary conditions, which are, as many political scientists note, characterised by the 'presidentialisation' of politics and the foregrounding of the leader under the gaze of the media. As the Conservative Party found in the 2017 UK general election, having a leader (Theresa May) who shied away from television debates, was uncomfortable with set-piece public speaking and unconvincing in front of cameras, is unlikely to advance the cause. Although the Conservatives won that election, many ascribed its dramatically reduced number of seats to Mrs May's less than compelling campaigning style.

From stability to crisis

For much of the time the appeal to the people is a rhetorical device used by politicians to bolster their claims so as to enjoy wide support for their policies. We might hear populist claims at election time, when the stakes are high in terms of engaging citizens and getting them mobilised to vote, but generally politics in democratic conditions has a more humdrum quality. It's a grey matter of 'who gets what, when, where and how', as Harold Lasswell's famously pithy summary puts it. It's not heroic. It doesn't stir the passions or fire the emotions. It just seeks to get stuff done. During times of crisis, however, populism takes on a different aspect.

In a crisis we are drawn to think less about the virtues of one politician or mainstream party over another and more about why things seem to be going wrong. High unemployment, recession, insecurity and social breakdown force us to reappraise not just the individual performance of politicians but how the system works, and for whom. It makes us examine the hegemonic structure of society, the core set of beliefs and values that underpin the society we live in. The more it looks to us as if there is some fundamental problem that needs to be fixed, the more it will appear that the differences between mainstream politicians are less important than what unites them. Differences that appeared significant during periods of stability seem trivial when the system itself is in question. Political parties merge, and candidates begin to look the same and sound the same; to be suit-wearing members of the 'elite'. They come to appear as part of the problem, rather than as part of the solution. 'No matter who you vote for, the government always gets in' to quote the inimitable Bonzo Dog Band.

A clear example of this transformation of thinking is the Occupy movement, and its resounding slogan 'We are the 99%'. The slogan challenges the pluralist account of how democracy functions, one that insists that under democratic conditions we can find representatives of every interest and every section of society. The suggestion is that our representatives are in league with the 1%, the rich and powerful whose needs carry far more weight than the rest of the world. It's a powerful slogan, and a populist one in this reading. But it would have had little purchase unless recession and austerity had forced a reappraisal of the basic values and expectations that underpin society. It wasn't Occupy that generated crisis but crisis that generated Occupy.

As the doubts multiply, we see a proliferation of populist initiatives, including new social movements and new political parties, whose principal claim is to challenge the elites, promising to fix things from outside. In the context of recession and austerity, it is unsurprising to find audiences becoming more receptive to outsider or populist parties. The global financial crisis undermined the hegemonic consensus that operated from the early 1980s to the first decade of the twenty-first century. It questioned the centrality of neo-liberalism, which permitted the left's critique of financialisation and inequality, and the embrace of globalisation to promote economic growth, the aspect latched on to by far-right or nativist political movements and parties. But none of this made much sense or had much traction with electorates during the stable period before the global financial crisis. Crisis permitted both the querying of the underpinning hegemonic logic and the elites who derived their power and privilege from it.

‸   This sounds like an account that stems from an economic grievance point of view but need not be read like that. The claim is more that the emergence of a discourse pitting the people against the elites is a sign of a fundamental schism developing, an uncoupling of citizens from those who are supposed to represent them; a symptom of a breakdown in the feedback loop that democracy was designed to sustain. This might be because the elites are inflicting policies on an unwilling populace but it may also be because the values and norms promoted by the elites fail to find favour with citizens or to reflect wider social grievances. In other words, crisis might be a symptom of cultural and democratic grievance just as much of economic grievance. It is not only impoverishment that is capable of feeding discontent but also social and cultural alienation from elite values.

Democracy after populism

With crisis comes the opportunity to challenge and then reconstitute the hegemonic basis of society. Crisis does not constitute the end of the world. It does not have to lead to social breakdown or disintegration. Rather, it forces a reconsideration of the terms and conditions of social life; people look for a change, for something better. Laclau offers the example of the birth of the welfare state in the UK after World War II as an illustration of such a shift. A hugely successful wartime leader, Winston Churchill, was defeated in the 1945 general election by a less heralded Labour politician, Clement Attlee. People were hungry to get away from post-war austerity and embrace a social system based on a more egalitarian and redistributive ethic. Churchill stood for a return to the past; Attlee for a new social order, the welfare state. When, in the 1970s, UK inflation went through the roof and world oil prices rose, the welfare model itself came under pressure, precipitating a further shift, away from the welfare state and towards neo-liberalism and the new public management.

This illustrates an important facet of Laclau's understanding of how populism works. There is no guarantee that, on the back of social crisis, the electorate will favour progressive or leftist solutions. On the contrary, citizens must be compelled by new positions and new solutions must be argued for. Arguments that might have had very little traction before crisis now have an audience that may well be more receptive to outsider or heterodox ideas. With self-organisation, a clear strategy articulated by a charismatic leader, and policies designed to address the immediate concerns of citizens who might have been seriously touched by austerity or injustice, democratic renewal may result.

Laclau's thinking about populism not only challenges mainstream commentary, which tends to focus on the negative effects of populism, but also the stance of many progressive activists who want to push democracy in a more egalitarian and participatory direction. Not all activists are comfortable with, or want to endorse, the idea of reviving or renewing democracy by embracing populism and investing in a charismatic figure. This, too, is Laclau's point: many activists are more comfortable demonstrating, occupying or protesting in the street than competing directly for power in elections. They may seek to develop a 'prefigurative' style of politics that enacts the kind of horizontal, leaderless forms of organisation they feel 'real democracy' should be about. Or they may feel that party-based organising is, in some other way, surrendering to 'the system'.

In Spain, the creation of *Podemos* and the elections of Ada Colau and Manuela Carmena took place in such a swirl of claim and counter-claim. But Laclau's point, deployed by left populists in Spain, Greece and elsewhere, is that during moments of crisis, opportunities come along to shift the boundaries of democratic participation and more generally, address some of the causes that have traditionally animated those on the left by the creation of a party or movement that will directly contest the hegemony of existing political forces. Such moments can – and should – be used to push for the greater good and for an enhancement of democracy in the name of the people.

Before leaving this section, I should perhaps make clear that the claim is not that every populist initiative is good for democracy; it's that populism is not necessarily bad for, or a threat to, democracy in the manner portrayed in classic accounts. Whether any populist initiative or movement will or will not prove a threat to democracy has nothing to do with whether it is *populist*. Populism, according to Laclau, is not a type of regime, or a particular vision of how we should live. Rather, it is an approach that sees politics as dynamic and influenced by wider social and economic influences. Democracy is a shifting and evolving set of practices and institutions, itself subject to debate and discussion. The only given is, as it were, that 'the people' authorise democracy. They are both its subject and its sovereign; without them there can be no democracy. Populism remains faithful to this idea, which is why Laclau says we cannot deny that populism is inextricably part of democratic life. It is the attempt to eliminate the centrality of the people in the process of legitimating and animating democracy that should concern us.

If there were a threat to democracy under contemporary conditions, it would not be populism but rather technocratic forms of governance that insist on closing deliberation on matters of public interest, due to their complexity. How often have we heard the sentiment that there's little point in engaging with citizens in a certain set of issues because it's 'too complex', because we 'wouldn't understand' or because we're 'not interested'? The corollary is that governance is best left to experts, to those who know how things work and who can articulate the public interest without the need to bother the public itself. It's for this reason that technocrats dread referendums; temporarily (at least) they lose control of the agenda. Populists, by contrast, are said to favour referendums because they offer a direct and unmediated expression of the 'will of the people', which plays into the hands of those who wish to circumscribe or avoid entanglement with institutions and processes. This may be an accurate representation of the thought processes of some populist leaders but it betrays a technocratic sensibility and a desire to maintain the elites' grip on the policy process and the system of governance. This feeds the thought that the elites are a separate and privileged caste operating according to their own needs and interests, rather than one whose power comes from the people.

A tale of two populisms

Is populism a threat to democracy? The first consideration is whether we see populism as an externality acting on democracy, as described by the critics of populism or as something internal to the logic of democratic contestation, in line with Laclau's arguments.

Most commentators agree that we need reference to a crisis to understand the predicament that we find ourselves in, and by extension why outsider movements and parties are gaining traction. But at the same time, as we know, the dominant view is that populism still represents a distinctive politics, whose pursuit will undermine pluralism, democratic institutions, civility, the free press and so on. A crisis just makes it easier for populists to establish themselves as credible alternatives to the political mainstream. The image conjured up is one in which an anti-democratic force arises from democracy itself.

Put in these rather reductive terms, we have an account that starts from an assumption that the system is stable and working well and that the elites are managing society in accordance with our needs and interests. Then, a movement or leader emerges that seems to threaten to overturn the system in the name of the people. The call goes out to defend society against the populist threat. The message is clear: we the democrats must resist the populists and defend our values and beliefs against those who threaten them. For lovers of western films, this is what we might call the *Rio Bravo* version of the populist threat; an easy-to-digest story, with clearly-labelled good guys and bad guys.

Another metaphor is of populism as a bacterium that has infected an otherwise healthy body. This plays to the idea, deeply rooted in the history of political thought, of the collective as a kind of organism, what used to be called the 'body politic'. In contemporary accounts, the body of democracy has been invaded by microbes or parasites that feed on it for their own benefit. If the body does not generate enough antibodies to repel the invaders or if the autoimmune system is too weak, it will wither and die.

Remaining with these analogies, let's imagine that in the western the drama centres on a village that is regularly raided by the local *bandidos*. The peasant inhabitants (the 99%) work hard to make ends meet but everything they earn is taken from them by a bunch of good-for-nothing robbers who possess the monopoly on the use of force (the 1%). How can they escape this vicious circle? The peasants decide that salvation can only be delivered in concert with outsiders. They head off to find some folks who will help. They return with a ramshackle group of rebels, led by a charismatic figure, to challenge the *bandidos* and restore justice. What do we have? Keen western-watchers will notice a passing resemblance to *The Magnificent Seven*. Same genre, different plot-line. The difference? The idea that an outside force is needed to remedy an unjust situation.

In the metaphor of the body, an appropriate counter-analogy might be of a man who is suffering a chronic illness and finds himself on a life support machine. His doctor reports that without a radical intervention his chances are slim. Without intervention, he probably won't pull through. But, the doctor says, there's a powerful medicine that might revive him; she's not sure it will work but his underlying condition means the risk is, in her view, well worth taking. This is the principle of chemotherapy: a powerful but potentially toxic substance is introduced into the body, to bring about improvement and hopefully a return to full health.

These analogies draw our attention to the centrality of crisis, or a sense of emergency, for how we might think about populism, why it appears and what its possible effects might be. If we think contemporary democracy is fundamentally healthy, that it functions in the best interests of citizens or perhaps that it cannot be improved on ('the least worst form of government', to slightly misquote Winston Churchill), populism will appear as a scourge, no matter the ideological disposition of any particular movement or party. If, however, our perception is that the system is less than healthy, that it is marked by injustice and that those who are in charge are incompetent, inefficient or acting in their own interests rather than the interests of society, populism takes on a different complexion. Depending on our values and orientation, we may feel that without a dose of outsider politics, nothing will change. The crisis will continue, and the threat of social breakdown will loom.

Where we end up in this debate tends to reflect where we started. If we are primarily interested in documenting what populism *is*, it's easy to conclude that populism is distinct from democracy, and not in a good way. It looks different, sounds different and *is* different, compared to ordinary, common-or-garden democratic politics. It's noisier, more boisterous, more passionate and more confronting. Naturally enough, on this basis, populism looks like a threat to democracy.

However, if we are interested in *why* populism arises, we may well end at a quite different conclusion. When we ask why, we are drawn towards the crisis afflicting democratic societies. Populism looks less like a threat to democracy and more like a response to the crisis. When things seem to be falling apart, people become receptive to parties and movements that promise a fresh start. Whether that 'something new' results in an improvement largely depends on whether we agree with the analysis of the particular party or movement in question, in particular their analysis of the weakness and deficiencies of the system. Certainly, some – but not all – populists have a rather underhand or duplicitous relationship with democracy. Indeed, some populist movements and parties have been inspired by well-aired and widely-shared grievances about how, and for whom, contemporary democracy functions. This brings us neatly to a second important consideration: do we think there are significant differences between populisms of the far right and populisms of the radical left?

What is noticeable in the approach of many who argue that populism is a threat to democracy is the *implicit* and occasionally *explicit* repudiation of the difference between movements and parties of the far right and those on the left. 'Implicit repudiation' involves using 'populism' to cover both the left and right varieties but only referring to right-wing examples, so that left-wing varieties are covered by association, rather than by direct reference. This tendency is particularly marked in the media, in which populism has, to all intents and purposes, become a synonym for far-right, authoritarian, nativist, anti-immigrant and racist parties. When we hear about the 'populist insurgency', the 'populist threat', the 'tide of populism' and so on, much of the time the writer has in mind authoritarian movements of the right. This can also be a feature of the populism studies literature, which tends to draw predominantly on examples from far-right movements and parties to illustrate what it takes to be the nature of populism. Far-right populism is, for one thing, more prevalent than left-wing populism. It's also been around longer, notwithstanding the Russian *Narodniks*.

To take one example, I have discussed more than once how leadership is portrayed in populist parties as being based on a cult of personality. The inference is that the party is subordinate to the leader, the reverse of the case in the political mainstream. This is very broadly true when it comes to far-right parties such as Wilders' Party for Freedom or Le Pen's National Rally but it doesn't hold up as well for populist parties of the far left. *Podemos* has, for most of its brief history, had a leadership triumvirate (more recently a duumvirate), to avoid the concentration of power in one person. *Syriza* is a coalition of forces largely held together by the diplomacy and pragmatism of Tsipras, not qualities normally associated with populists. If, for the sake of the argument, we include Corbyn and Sanders as populists (as the media tends to do), the evidence still looks weak. Sanders has a following in the Democratic Party but was unable to win the nomination against an establishment candidate. Corbyn certainly has developed a loyal following, particularly amongst the young and those new to politics, but his parliamentary colleagues itch for the moment when they can depose him and return to a more 'sensible' mainstream leader.

There are two types of response to these issues. First, we can argue that the dominant account of populism is too narrowly drawn, and we need to recognise that populism represents little threat to democracy. Second, we can be more explicit about what kind of populism we are discussing when we look at how parties and movements are likely to affect the societies in which they arise.

This second concern has led several specialists to clarify their use of the term populism, to avoid confusion. Pippa Norris, for example, makes clear in her discussion in *Cultural Backlash* that she is interested in 'authoritarian populism', distinguished from liberal or left-wing populisms on the basis that there are significant differences between the far right and the radical left, both in terms of values and of goals and objectives. It's a telling gesture. In her view populism is not itself authoritarian but rather, can readily be paired with authoritarianism to produce a particular politics. This implies that populism could be paired with, say, liberalism (for example in the case of President Macron) to produce a very different kind of politics, a kind that offers little or no threat to democracy – or indeed which helps bolster it against anti-democratic forces.

'Explicit repudiation', by contrast, is an approach that sees no substantial difference between far right and far left, and thus that populism can be used to describe them all. UKIP and *Podemos*, Farage and Iglesias are two sides of the same coin. They're all as bad as each other and they're all a threat to democracy. Why? Because they're outsiders, not mainstream parties. They're critical of the status quo. They want to change the nature and feel of the political system from open, pluralist and tolerant to closed, monist and intolerant, usually with a charismatic figurehead who claims to know what the people want before the people themselves do. In this reading, populism has an 'inner logic' or tacit ideology that drives politics in a certain direction: away from democracy.

The difficulty is finding cases to fit the analysis. While much of the description resonates with right-wing populisms, the evidence is thinner when applied to contemporary left-wing cases. Certainly, there are examples in the developing world of left-wing leaders demonstrating authoritarian tendencies, such as Chávez in Venezuela. But evidence from advanced democracies is harder to come by. Some worry, for example, about what they see as the undermining of internal democracy in Jeremy Corbyn's Labour Party by the mobilisation of supporter groups such as Momentum to deselect sitting MPs and replace them with more radical candidates. Jean-Luc Mélenchon is also regularly accused of demagogic or messianic tendencies by the French media, and *La France Insoumise* can seem like an extension of his personal profile, such is his apparent domination of its messaging and approach. But left populist figures in power have yet to show an appetite for authoritarian practices, for closing independent institutions or subjugating civil society through the extension of police powers, as right-wing figures such as Viktor Orbán have. Is it a matter of time before they do? Can we expect left populisms to develop the same intolerance for democracy as those on the right?

Perhaps. But for the present the evidence is weak. And it's weak for a reason: the recent rise of left populism can, at least in part, be traced to the view that democracy has been undermined by clientelism, cronyism and corruption and therefore needs to be strengthened and made more meaningful. If there is some sort of hidden agenda to subvert or threaten democracy, populists are doing a fine job of disguising their true intentions. If their true intention is to weaken or undermine democracy, we can expect a backlash both from their supporters and from citizens at the ballot box. If we have learned one thing from the rise of populist movements and parties, it's that citizens are quick to turn on politicians who don't deliver what they promised or who abuse their trust. A left populist party that attacked fundamental freedoms, that left clientelism in place, that failed to address the causes of austerity, is unlikely to hold on to its supporters. So far then, contemporary left populisms appear to emerge from a different basis to right populisms, have different aims and objectives and call on different social forces for support. In short, calling a party or movement 'populist' doesn't tell us much about its values, outlook and beliefs.

This leads us to a final possibility, which I have been discussing in the second half of this chapter in my consideration of Laclau's contribution. 'The people' is the subject of democratic politics and the sole basis for authorising and legitimising what is done in its name. This implies populism has no specific content. It does not describe a set of outcomes, policies or positions that would enable us to say this is right and this is left. Rather, it is a form of politics that speaks to the people in the name of the people, as a way of garnering support for a political project.

Populism *can* be a threat to democratic values and processes, but it could equally be a means for the *expansion* of democracy. Since, for Laclau, there is no way for a political strategy to gain traction without being populist, it follows that populism itself is neither democratic nor undemocratic. It's just how claims are articulated under democratic conditions. Those claims might be authoritarian or nativist, or they might be the demand for a more open and pluralist form of democracy. There is no other way the demand for the renewal of democracy could be articulated effectively, that is as a means of garnering support for a party or movement, *except* on the basis of the populist claim that the people need or want more democracy.

This runs counter to how populism is discussed in much of the mainstream media. For them, populism is threatening because it stands for ideas, movements and leaders outside the mainstream. For Laclau, populism is neither 'inside' nor 'outside'; it is just how we advance claims under democratic conditions. It becomes 'outside' when it is allied to the idea of the elites working in opposition to the needs and interests of 'the people'. But there are many different narratives of how the elites have let us down. Might any of these movements or parties prove a threat to democracy?

They might. However, it won't be because they're populist. It will be because they pursue policies that shut down debate, threaten institutions and deny basic civil liberties. Populism is a strategy for winning and holding power, not a prescription or guide to what happens with power. That resides with the values and beliefs of the movement or party using a populist strategy, not with populism itself.

Conclusion

The issue of whether populism is a threat to democracy is clearly pressing. Naturally, talk of a populist insurgency makes us want to understand the nature of the underlying threat. As we have seen, that threat is clear and present as far as mainstream opinion is concerned, and certainly as far as much of the media are concerned. How could it not be when, by definition, populism represents a break in the democratic circuit? Populism is a form of outsider politics; it sets the people against the elites, those charged with running the system.

Notwithstanding the dominance of accounts of populism that see it as a threat to democracy, to help us think about the causes of populism as well as what we should do about it, it's possible, and perhaps necessary, to frame the issue in a more capacious way. Perhaps we should cease to see populism as something that 'they' are attracted to, that outsiders display, that only appeals to the margin. Crisis is producing populisms. It's pushing citizens to look for hope, if not redemption. With crisis comes opportunity, as old truths and ways of doing things come under scrutiny. Populism can help advance the cause of democratic renewal or it can play into the hands of those with much less benign purposes. It does not dictate a particular kind of outcome or a specific vision; rather, it determines a certain type of political strategy based on mobilising citizens behind the idea of change or renewal.

Threat or renewal? How we respond to the question will be shaped not just by the definitions and approaches of different schools of thought but by whether we feel the populist critique is justified and whether the solutions parties and movements offer are likely to lead to positive outcomes. This is not quite the same as saying that 'it's just your point of view'. It's more that the answer will depend on our perception of how well democracy is doing.

This perception is often shaped by where we are in relation to where power lies in our societies. If we are beneficiaries of current structures, we may well feel much less urgency about the need for change than those who feel themselves hard done by, without a job, denied a pension or lacking much of a voice. Crisis looks different and feels different depending on how well we are doing and what our prospects look like. People like me, with comfortable permanent jobs, may well be concerned about the boisterous anti-establishment message of populism. By contrast people who have been evicted from their home or been made redundant might well wonder 'what have those in power ever done for me?'

This reminds us that for all the talk of populism as a *cause* of crisis, as a stirrer of passions and emotions, we don't get very far in understanding it without referring to feelings of loss, powerlessness, insecurity and precariousness. Populism didn't invent the conditions that generate such feelings, even if it feeds on them. Take crisis away and populism loses energy and momentum. Extravagant or emotive appeals to the people sound excessive. But put threat, fear and a sense of alienation from the political class into the mix, stir it with an increasingly shrill mediatisation of the issues that confront us, and the likelihood of populism gaining ground increases dramatically. Perceptions are everything; how our perceptions are shaped and by whom has quickly become a vital matter for everyone interested in the current direction of politics. It's a complex matter, rendered more complex still by the 'new media galaxy' created by the proliferation of digital technologies that greatly enhance the capacity of all sorts of people, not just the elites, to project their message, influence opinion and produce unexpected outcomes. Is this profound change in the ecology of the media, in who makes information, with what tools and for what purposes, making it harder to discern what is true and what is false? Are we becoming playthings for powerful interests seeking to use crises for nefarious purposes? Is our new era of post-truth undermining democracy and leading the way for populists, of whatever stripe, to take over?

5

Is populism a variety of 'post-truth politics'?

Since the populist insurgency of 2016 many commentators and analysts have taken a great interest in 'post-truth'; the emergence of a culture of systematic lying, deceit, fraud and fake news. The insurgent events seem to be linked to the emergence of political figures and movements that challenge the veracity of established positions, experts and received wisdom across a range of issues. This is not simply an insurgency against a particular style of politics; it's an insurgency against the understandings that have informed our view of politics, about what the priorities of our governments should be, about the nature of the world being created by globalisation and about the wisdom of large flows of people, to name just a few areas that once seemed uncontentious.

Populism has introduced a more combative style of politics that not only challenges arguments and rival positions but also claims they are untrue. It does so both by challenging facts and producing alternative 'facts' when they are needed or desired. Trump's campaign was marked by all manner of allegations against Hillary Clinton, based·on what seemed the flimsiest of evidence, inflated into grotesque 'truths' by supportive elements of the media and indeed by their overt manipulation, orchestrated by supporters such as Steve Bannon, who became Trump's chief strategist. The Leave campaign in the Brexit referendum notoriously emblazoned claims across advertising hoardings and buses about the amount of money that would be brought back from the EU, and the fresh influx of immigrants that would happen in the event of a 'remain' vote.

On inspection, many of these 'facts' were shown to be fanciful. Yet they stuck and became part of the background of claims and counterclaims that marked increasingly contentious campaigns. What interested commentators was the brazen manipulation. Never in the context of democratic debate, it seemed, had political figures and organisations fabricated statistics in such an egregious fashion. These were no mere exaggerations or distortions of a kind familiar in previous election campaigns. Backed by supportive media outlets, they were the production of untruths that were calculated to stick, be accepted and acted on by the public.

This has been taken as evidence that we have entered an era of 'post-truth politics'. This has, it is argued, both novel and calamitous consequences. Democracies rely on honesty, integrity and openness to the testing of claims and counterclaims to make those who govern accountable. Take truth away, manipulate data, peddle falsehoods and we lose the qualities that mark democracies as guardians of what the philosopher Karl Popper memorably termed 'the open society'.

The key question is the nature of the connection between these developments and the emergence of populism. Is populism driving us towards a post-truth politics? Are Trump, Farage, Le Pen and their ilk behind this dramatic evolution in the nature and style of politics? Is the emergence of post-truth politics resulting in support for and the encouragement of populist initiatives? Or are both caused by some other factor lying behind our scepticism towards the establishment, experts and, more broadly, authority.

The truth about post-truth

It's little coincidence that 'post-truth' was the Oxford English Dictionary's word of the year for 2016. Its fate seems inextricably bound up with the populist insurgency. However, 'post-truth' has been around rather longer; it was coined to describe the events around the Iran-Contra Scandal of the early 1990s. But only in the wake of the flagrant examples of truth-bending associated with the emergence of populist figures such as Trump and Farage has it really caught on, so why post-truth and not simple 'lying'? The point commentators want to make is that lying is episodic, whereas post-truth has an orientation to the truth.

Why do we lie? Because there is something to be gained from not telling the truth. Truth and lies are two sides of the same coin. 'Either she is lying or she is telling the truth.' How many times have we heard that phrase on television or at the cinema? But the comportment of Trump and others poses a rather different question, hence the need for a new term. The issue is disregard for the truth, about whether something really happened, about whether something costs x or y; the issue is the manner by which truth came to be subordinated to immediate and longer-term political goals.

Consider the Leave campaign's notorious Brexit battle bus. On it was emblazoned the claim that the UK would be £350 million a week better off by leaving the EU; proceeds that would be used to support the National Health Service. This was an attractive policy to many weary citizens. However, commentators pointed out that this figure discounted the amount that the UK *gets back* from the European Union, due not least to the efforts of previous Eurosceptics such as Mrs Thatcher. The battle bus should really have stated that the UK would be around £150 million better off. The precise sum of money isn't really the issue; the point remains the same. Britain should leave the European Union because it pays large sums of money to a foreign bureaucracy whose main function seems to be to develop ever more irritating ways of spending the cash of hard-pressed UK citizens.

Another example is Trump's 2017 reference to a terrorist attack in Sweden to justify limiting the number of refugees taken in as part of a package of measures to reassure Americans concerned about the increased threat from Islamic extremism. 'We've got to keep our country safe,' he told supporters at a rally in Florida. 'You look at what's happening in Germany, you look at what happened last night in Sweden… They took in large numbers. They're having problems like they never thought possible.' So far, so good, except that the terrorist attack never took place, as was immediately confirmed by Swedish government sources. This didn't matter to Trump and it didn't seem to matter to his supporters. Why? Because the message latent in the claim remained valid, as far as many were concerned. Sure, no attack took place in Sweden. Perhaps Trump confused it with Norway, Denmark or some other country. It hardly mattered: 'We know attacks of this kind take place everywhere and we need to be super-vigilant about taking the steps needed to prevent them from happening in the USA.' To Trump's opponents it was a flagrant lie; to his supporters, and indeed quite possibly to Trump himself, it was a mistake, an oversight, a mild exaggeration, or a fatigue-induced slip that nonetheless was valid, because it pointed at a real problem. It might have been an outright lie but in a context where the function of truth is to serve larger political purposes, we have lost touch with the idea of lying as the conscious act of not telling the truth.

These examples illustrate important features of 'post-truth'. It has a different quality to lying; lying implies a certain precision, knowingness and sense of intent to deceive. 'Post-truth' describes a world in which anyone can say whatever they want if it serves their needs and purposes. Honesty and integrity decline as virtues we want in our leaders, in favour of effectiveness, impact and charisma.

How has it come to this? How have we arrived at a situation in which citizens are happy to support politicians, public figures and campaigns that have a cavalier disregard for the truth?

Are post-modernism and relativism to blame?

A persistent refrain from critics of post-truth is that academics and intellectuals, the traditional guardians of knowledge, have done their best, from their privileged position in the ivory towers of elite universities, to undermine the objectivity of truth. These critics are getting at the popularity of a particularly sceptical branch of the humanities: 'post-modernism'. Post-modernism is associated with a group of exotic-sounding French thinkers of the middle of the twentieth century, figures such as Jacques Derrida, Jean-François Lyotard and Michel Foucault, all of whom still enjoy exalted reputations. They took their cue from the nihilistic philosophy of Friedrich Nietzsche, famous for his pithy aphorism 'God is dead!'

Nietzsche was unapologetically sceptical about truth claims. The truth is, he said, no more than 'a mobile army of metaphors'. This implies that what we take to be true is not grounded in objective reality but in the force, or persuasiveness, of language. Moreover, the strong create the truth, and they do so to justify their values and worldview. In this sense, the truth of a statement is more a function of the ends it serves than the reality it describes. Sounds quite a lot like Trump and his Swedish terrorism story.

For his French interlocutors, Nietzsche's insight into the relationship between truth and power came to underpin some variety or another of relativism, or so they claimed. Derrida developed a philosophy that stresses how language, and by extension truth, works through the 'play of difference' between terms, as opposed to mapping an objective reality. Lyotard famously coined the term 'the post-modern condition' to describe the world around him in the 1970s, a world marked by 'incredulity towards metanarratives'; loss of faith in the objective quality of the sciences, ideologies, religion. Foucault urged intellectuals to drop their obsession with universal or objective truths in favour of a historical method that shows how truth is constructed to serve particular needs.

For post-modernism's critics, this encourages scepticism about objectivity and the distinction between true and false accounts of reality. Everything is reduced to mere narrative. Whoever is able to spin the most persuasive, most attractive, story establishes themselves as a truth-teller. Bullshit goes unexamined, claims are untested, facts lie unchecked. Generations of students have been taught that there is no objective reality and they need to concentrate on style and the arts of persuasion through rhetorical flourish. Truth becomes whatever we want it to be. Post-modernism and relativism are therefore complicit in creating an atmosphere of scepticism about truth. We've lost the appetite to challenge lies on the basis that there is a truth or a reality against which to measure the veracity of any given statement. We are helpless before 'post-truth'.

Undeniably, this is compelling. There's little doubt that arguments such as these are rehearsed daily in the quads and cloisters of many of our renowned universities, where truth claims are tested and students encouraged to take a critical stance in relation to knowledge. However, there's a danger not only of exaggerating the impact of intellectual trends and tendencies but also confusing causes and effects.

Regarding their impact, post-modernism and relativism may well be fashionable in a small corner of the humanities but ideas such as these were long ago pooh-poohed in other parts of the academy. There are few post-moderns in engineering or medical faculties. Positivism and the scientific method reign largely unquestioned across the sciences and social sciences; as the T-shirt puts it, 'Science doesn't care what you believe!' If we are looking for sources of scepticism and self-doubt, it is unlikely to be found in today's technologically- and vocationally-oriented universities.

On causes and effects, the subtitle of Lyotard's infamous book *The Postmodern Condition* should alert us to the nature of the claims inside: *A Report on Knowledge*. It's a report on how scepticism and relativism became implanted in our thinking. Scepticism towards theology ('God is dead!') has spread to scepticism towards other kinds of 'metanarrative', such as Marxism leading us to what Lyotard playfully termed a kind of 'paganism'. Post-modernism is a condition, a state of mind, a comportment towards the world shared by citizens who no longer believe in the ultimate reality or grounding of ideologies, or even of science.

From this point of view, it would be more accurate to say that post-modernists are chroniclers of the decline of objective truth, rather than advocates for relativising the truth. Blaming post-modernism for increased scepticism towards the truth is like blaming a warning light for an engine fault. The light is not the cause of the fault; the 'fault' is the emergence of increased scepticism towards received truths, towards the idea of God, the divine right of kings, the objectivity of the Bible and the 'natural order', none of which were produced by the 'light', that is, by post-modernism.

A further point to bear in mind is that querying 'facts' was once celebrated as part of the legacy of the Renaissance, the Enlightenment and, ironically, the democratic revolutions of the eighteenth and nineteenth centuries. Modernity was built on scepticism and doubt about the nature of the external world, translated into a deep curiosity to understand the place of the Earth in the solar system, the circulation of blood in the body, the justification for the monarchy, and so on. Far from post-modernism being something that undermines traditions and approaches intrinsic to scientific, technological and social progress, there's a reasonable case for seeing it as in keeping with them. Without scepticism we are in thrall to fundamentalism and to the high priests of Truth, whether religious or (pseudo-)scientific.

Is expert knowledge dead?

What the post-modernists really want to claim is that we are collectively becoming more sceptical and less impressed by the claims of 'experts', no matter how well-qualified, prestigious or seemingly superior in their understanding of the world.

Going back to Nietzsche, part of his case is that in the transition from feudal and pre-feudal societies to modernity we move from societies based on and organised by religious orthodoxy to ones based on the secular ideal of scepticism towards truth claims, including the claim that there is some ultimate ground of truth. Once, this seemed helpful in terms of generating the practices that we associate with scientific progress. Popper, for example, argued that science would be impossible in closed societies where certain 'truths' are shielded from scrutiny. Science depends on our ability to subject all facts, all forms of truth, all propositions to test. Take that away, and we are back with the mysticism of religious belief, political theology and all the rest.

This is a double-edged sword, for what are scientists if not a species of expert? Here lies one of the paradoxes of our age. Scepticism towards the truth is helpful, because it encourages us to continually examine and re-examine the propositions by which we live, and to adopt new and better ones when those propositions are shown to be deficient or false. Thus we achieve scientific progress and, more broadly, social progress, according to philosophers such as Popper. The problem is that this also encourages scepticism about propositions that, for whatever reason, we might feel should be defended in the name of a higher end or goal. The classic contemporary example of this paradox is climate change.

According to the vast majority of scientists working in the field, evidence of the impact of human activity on the climate is incontrovertible. Given what is at stake, we therefore need to set aside our doubts and get on with enacting measures and policies that will keep future temperature rises to a minimum. The threat of environmental catastrophe should, in other words, trump the practice of regarding facts as contingent propositions which may or may not turn out to be true when tested further. We need to accept – as fact – that unless we change our ways the planet will not survive in a state that allows human existence. Constantly pandering to the sceptics who insist on doubting the reality of climate change is to condemn the planet and ourselves to oblivion.

The war on experts and truth has consequences that go far beyond the usual political point-scoring. In this view, we don't choose what to believe on the basis of the facts; rather, we choose the facts that accord with our values and beliefs. If an expert says something that accords with our worldview, we are happy to respect their position, training and learning, but if they offer facts that conflict with how we see things, they become one of those contemptible 'experts' we should be suspicious of. For those who love driving around in monster 4x4s, flying long distances for thirty-minute meetings and having the air con going all day, it's irritating to be told that this is imperilling the planet. As the bumper sticker says: 'Climate Change: It Used to be Called Weather!' For those who don't 'believe' in climate change, no amount of evidence will change their minds. Pictures of starving polar bears or huge glaciers crashing into the sea will not convince them that we are in any way to blame. Just more 'fake news' generated by those damned 'experts' to justify their research grants and cushy academic positions.

The facility to pick and choose who or what to believe, to turn the facts on their head, is very much in evidence in today's populist political discourse. Michael Gove, one of the UK's leading Brexiteers, denounced the Treasury economists for their continued negativity in relation to the likely economic consequences of the UK leaving the European Union. Their claims did not accord with his worldview, and his belief in the need for Britain to 'take back control', so he dismissed them with the wave of a hand. Trump denounces not just climate change but environmental impacts more generally. He urges the rejection of free trade on the grounds that America is 'getting smashed', notwithstanding the experts' view that the USA has been both the principal driver of economic globalisation and its principal beneficiary.

'Confirmation bias' is important for understanding this inter-play between facts and values. Given contestation over the facts of climate change, the impact of globalisation, the nature of trade and so on, we tend to follow our own beliefs. We select the facts that fit with our worldview, rather than letting our worldview be determined by facts.

The individualisation of truth claims is consistent more gen-erally with how sociologists view the erosion of authority, tradi-tion and received wisdom as part of modernity's tendency to put truth in play. Nothing new; this tendency was not only noticed by Nietzsche but also, for example, by Karl Marx. Describing the world being created in the 1840s by the dramatic impact of capi-talism and globalisation, Marx was moved to note that 'all that is solid melts into air. All that is holy is profaned and man is at last compelled to face with sober senses his real conditions of life and his relations with his kind'. Marx expected that, with the erosion of received wisdoms, of religion and ideology more generally, we would be able to see the 'real' reality as it was: capitalist exploita-tion at the hands of the bourgeois class.

So much for the end of ideology. The erosion of inherited understandings has led not to the consecration of a singular truth, as Marx hoped, but to a broader mistrust of truth and those who claim to know the truth, whether they be climate scientists, economists, politicians or Communist Party *apparatchiks*. We have 'individualised' truth. We have made truth a matter of personal validation through experience and emotion. 'Do I *think* it's true?'

'Does it accord with my experience of how things work?' 'Are things better than they used to be?'

⟍ If our own experience of the world helps us to select facts and our political positions, we shouldn't be surprised that today's politics is often built on a turning away from the complexity of the current world towards a nostalgia for the solidity and certainties of the past. More comforting to find solace in tales of how we will recover a past that was simpler, purer and less complicated, than trying to make our way through thickets of competing explanations. Populism thrives on the desire for a simplification of the world, a narrowing of complexity to a few easy-to-remedy tasks, and on offering a vision, often nostalgic, of a world in which order has been restored. 'Sort France Out', 'Take Back Control', 'Make America Great Again'. Simple gestures, built on simple truths, and even simpler solutions.

Has the Internet made it more difficult to separate fact from fiction?

A key factor for those seeking to explain the rise of post-truth is the impact of digital technology on how we view the world, how we process information and how those who wish to influence us can do so without our knowledge or engagement. Before the Internet our understanding of the world was transmitted through published materials and mass media, dominated by a small number of players, including the state. Given the costs of production it was the elites who determined what we saw, read and watched.

The Internet changed all this. The monopoly on knowledge exercised by a small number of media outlets, universities and suchlike institutions has been rudely overturned by a proliferation of news sources, blog posts, YouTube videos, Facebook posts, tweets and so on. From being the responsibility of the few, knowledge-creation became an activity that anyone could indulge in, with all the risks and opportunities this implies.

Until quite recently this change was regarded with great enthusiasm by 'techno-Utopians' who looked forward to the creation of a new 'knowledge society' along flatter, less hierarchical lines. They foresaw a democratisation of knowledge, in which sharing information from all manner of sources would enable us to build a clearer picture of what was going on around us. As sources of news and information multiplied, so we would gain a better sense of the world than we could during the era of the lone news reporter. This could only add to our understanding and stimulate better, more engaged solutions to our problems. It would lead to more open, more transparent decision-making, as the claims of those in power were scrutinised with much greater efficacy than before. If 'knowledge is power', the greater circulation of knowledge among citizen networks could only increase the power of citizens to influence and determine what is done in their name.

In *The Net Delusion* Evgeny Morozov vividly documented how hopes that the Internet would blow the lid off the otherwise hidden world of dictatorships, despotisms and tyrannies around the world were raised. It would provide a means to connect, to share stories, to form groups and ultimately to challenge monopolies, whether informational or political. The Green Revolution in Iran during 2009 and 2010 gave us our first glimpse of a Twitter-led challenge to authority, closely followed in 2011 by the Arab Spring, #15M and Occupy. At the same time, WikiLeaks exposed the activity of diplomats and intelligence agencies, shining a light into a dark space, giving hope for a more transparent, more open style of governance. The world seemed, as Paul Mason put it, to be 'kicking off', to be exploding from the sheer potential energy unleashed by the digital revolution.

The techno-Utopians expected the Internet to explode monopolies on truth and power. The techno-cynics warned of a different kind of potential: the power to generate stories, material and content designed not to enlighten but to generate revenue on the one hand and aid certain political outcomes on the other. Those with short attention spans and a limited desire to engage with the complexity of the real world took the 'clickbait' of cynical operators looking to make a quick buck. Often, the best means of generating traffic proved to be 'fake news' that offered a dramatic spin on a conventional wisdom, whether it be conspiracy theories about 9/11, the birthplace of Barack Obama or climate science; critiques of whatever anyone held to be 'fact'. The Internet provided a perfect platform for every cause, no matter how far-fetched. Prejudices bloomed in the virgin territory of a largely unregulated virtual environment. The weirder and wilder the story, the more clicks, the more influence, the more money.

One effect of these new media is the development of 'echo chambers', in which those with a mutual hostility or interest can congregate without fear of challenge. Think that Obama is really related to Osama? Here's a forum, a website, a chat room in which you can hang out with others who share your obsession and will reconfirm your beliefs. Far from the Internet driving us towards a single or unified view of the 'real' reality, the charge is that it does the opposite: it fosters the proliferation of micro-communities of fellow travellers with mutually-reinforcing beliefs and prejudices. Instead of forcing us to gather into a global conversation about how the world works and what we can collectively do to improve it, the Internet pushes us into increasingly distinct silos, tribes and groups that confirm our biases while permitting us to remain blissfully detached from other viewpoints. The ability of the state or other traditional sources of authority to influence opinion and shape debate diminishes. The proliferation of Internet users, the breakdown of state monopolies on broadcasting and the decline of serious newspapers raise the stakes for knowledge creation and propagation. We are losing the anchor points of a shared understanding of reality,

The evidence, if not incontrovertible, certainly seems to point to a significant change in the nature of truth, of how it works, where it comes from, and how it circulates and implants itself. As my illustrations show, the transition from truth to post-truth certainly seems to assist populism in specific ways. A climate of scepticism of experts and other sources of authoritative opinion helps populists challenge establishment narratives, whether they be about the climate, globalisation or migration. Outsider views seem to thrive when the insider or establishment view no longer carries the weight it once did. Theories that might have seemed eccentric, bizarre or outlandish can gain traction under these new conditions and drive mainstream views on to the back foot.

Is post-truth new? The Internet has added new tools to the repertoire of those who wish to undermine confidence in authority but are we sure the manipulation of the truth and images, fake news, is novel? Are we confronting a new threat?

Truth, lies and politics: what's new?

Reading the reports on the development of post-truth, it's easy to form the impression that systematic lying and deception are new to politics. Or if not new then perhaps particular individuals lying to advance their own interests, or paper over some infelicity, mistake, or impropriety. The image of democratic politics the classic textbooks like to dwell on centres on the pursuit of the public interest, with our representatives, the politicians, acting with integrity and transparency to advance the collective good. It's instructive to remind ourselves that some of the classics of political thought can give us a different impression.

One of the oldest works in the canon of political thought, Plato's *Republic*, written around 400 BCE, gives a frank assessment of the centrality of lies to politics. Plato advocated what he termed a 'noble lie' to justify what otherwise might be regarded as unjustifiable: an unequal social order. His point was that only some people are fit to rule. Not everyone possesses good judgement, a sense of the common good and a love of truth; all parts of the *technē*, or technique of governance. Some have it, but most don't. How then to explain who should rule and who should obey? Should we just say, 'you're not smart enough to rule' and hope the listener is happy to agree? Unlikely to work. Plato's solution is for the elites to propagate a story about how some people are born with gold qualities, others with silver and the rest with bronze. Gold people have the intelligence, insight and integrity to rule as 'philosopher kings', silver people, or the guardians, should protect society, and everyone else should get on with the basic jobs. Assuming the lie was told consistently, and with the best interests of the people at heart, it should guarantee their support.

From the idea of a 'noble lie' it was a short step to the view of early modern theorists such as David Hume (1711–76) and Jean-Jacques Rousseau (1712–78), that every society needs some sort of 'foundation myth' to explain why some people rule and everyone else obeys, why we have monarchies, why some people are rich and other people are poor. The truth, if told, would take us into a dark realm of conquest, slavery and genocide, which would lead us to query the legitimacy of the existing order. Better, for everyone's sake, to paper over the dark side, with pragmatic tales of 'social contracts' being entered into and 'glorious' revolutions from an imagined popular insurrection.

Lies are needed, not just to paper over the origin of societies and political orders but also to defend the interests of the state, and by extension the people. The Florentine philosopher Niccolò Machiavelli (1469–1527), whose name became the popular adjective 'Machiavellian', used to describe politically cunning, if questionable, behaviour, insisted elites had a licence to lie, act unethically and generally set purity of purpose to one side to advance the needs and interests of the collective.

Sentiments such as these became the basis for the doctrines of *realpolitik* and *raison d'état* (reason of state) that became widely accepted in the early modern period. These doctrines argue that states and rulers cannot afford to be virtuous, or to let moral and ethical considerations dictate how they should act under all circumstances. Rather, they need to consider how to engineer the best possible outcome with the resources available. If that meant resorting to underhand methods, to lying or cheating, to advance the greater cause, then so be it.

Machiavelli's insights underpin what is today called a 'realist' view of how politics works. In a world of relentless competition for scarce resources, politics becomes a matter of mobilising everything at one's disposal to ensure the security and well-being of one's own group, nation or state. The people will love you not for being the most ethical leader, but for being the most effective leader. This means giving them what they want: money, health and security. Everything else can be regarded as a second order priority. If the military needs to use torture to extract confessions from would-be terrorists, so be it. If we need to suspend *habeas corpus* for foreign soldiers, too bad. If we need to cut ourselves loose from international protocols and obligations to further the national interest, bring it on. Failing to do so is to allow one's morals and values to threaten the security of the nation. What we need are 'wins', not plaudits for good behaviour from the United Nations.

Even these brief vignettes offer an insight into a mode of thinking that is surprisingly common, not just amongst political theorists but also amongst those who either practise politics or regularly comment on it. This is that politics is a deeply imperfect, or compromised, activity. It's built on lies in the form of foundation myths. Unethical and immoral activity is papered over where political goals are advanced. Truth and morality are held hostage to the greater needs of the state, to politicians' self-interest, to the need to shield citizens from difficult decisions with imperfect outcomes. It is for this reason that no modern politician is complete without a small army of 'spin doctors', who seek to show their candidate and their record in the best possible light, notwithstanding the inevitable blemishes, skeletons in the cupboard, infelicities and failures with which they might be associated. As experts often comment, politics has increasingly become a game of marketing, an alchemical task of turning imperfection, bullshit and mediocrity into 'gold', in the form of a successful candidate, policy or outcome.

From this point of view, Trump, Gove, Farage, Le Pen *et al* hardly represent a break from the inheritance of politics. Lying, cheating and grandiose claims are not at all new; rather part of the cut and thrust of political life. What perhaps is new is the casual indifference to being caught lying, exaggerating or inflating 'facts' to suit immediate political needs. But this need not be damaging in a context where the expectations are already set low for integrity in public life and where the public is receptive to a particular kind of political message.

When we half-expect our politicians to lie, cheat and otherwise behave according to the rules of the gutter, the onus is on them to do this with some flair, charisma and 'authenticity'. The public will apparently forgive major blemishes if they like the message; if it resonates with their needs and interests. As the USA-based journalist Salena Zito noted, when Trump speaks 'the press take him literally but not seriously; his supporters take him seriously but not literally'. This captures the issue in a nutshell. Trump is a worry for those who think public figures should be earnest, sincere folks committed to truth-telling no matter what. He's much less of a worry for those looking for an upbeat story about how the USA is going to get back on its feet.

None of these rules out politicians behaving ethically and even putting ethics at the forefront of their immediate concerns. It just means their performance must match the message. If one's view of the elites is that they have kowtowed to foreign interests, been weak and vacillated in the face of threats and terrorism, then one is hardly going to look askance at a leader whose main pitch is that we should do *anything*, including cheating, lying and permitting torture, if that increases the likelihood of winning.

Manipulating data, images and the historical record: a sordid past

Much of the power of the post-truth thesis lies in its depiction of a world in which we are lied to, claims are exaggerated, and these lies and exaggerations are visually and emotionally reinforced by the manipulation of data and images. Fake news sites pump out fabricated stories, using digital techniques to alter faces and places. YouTube channels mash up digital content to try to make us change our mind on an issue by convincing us that something happened or did not happen. Photos are altered to give favourable impressions, from the size of the crowd at Trump's inauguration to the thickness of his hair. The truth withers under the assault of digitally enabled activists promoting an alternative view of the world.

This is, undeniably, concerning. But to those with a passing interest in the evolution of news management and propaganda over the twentieth century, it has an all-too-familiar ring. Much of this resonance is associated with the development of authoritarian regimes keen to deploy new techniques and technologies to bolster their hold on power.

The Soviet regime of the 1920s understood the power of images to build a favourable impression in a context where its opponents often had the upper hand. The regime had no qualms about fabricating the historical record to burnish its image where necessary. A classic example was the Soviet regime's commissioning of the film-maker, Sergei Eisenstein, to put a gloss on the events of October 1917 when the Bolsheviks seized power.

The Bolsheviks understood that the story of a popular uprising gave their regime legitimacy, but the evidence did not fit. The 'storming' of the Winter Palace was anything but legitimate. The palace had in fact been abandoned by the previous regime; the attacking Bolsheviks were confronted by a squadron of poorly-equipped cadets. A few shots were fired before, in a matter of minutes, the cadets surrendered. It would be difficult to imagine anything that looked less like a mass popular insurgency. Eisenstein was therefore tasked with recreating the event; this time, a cast of thousands poured gloriously through the streets of St Petersburg in a gesture of democratic upsurge. The resulting film, *October*, was a big hit and helped to paint the Soviet regime in a much better light for its citizens.

The rewriting of history did not stop there. Stalin was particularly mindful of the fact that other leaders were more closely associated with these events than he was, and thus potential threats in terms of the affections of the party and the public. He therefore set about – literally – erasing the record of figures such as Trotsky and Bukharin, removing their faces from official photos taken to record the events of the revolution. Obliterating the evidence of their participation, while inflating his own, would naturally see his stock rise and theirs fall into a dark hole.

Mendacity and lying became art forms, literally and metaphorically, not only in the USSR but also in Nazi Germany. Both sought to construct a parallel reality to paper over the many cracks and imperfections of the real world. All newspapers were taken over by the state. All channels of public communication were unceasingly regulated. Every kind of public discourse with any political content came under intense scrutiny. Books were removed from libraries; many were burned or erased from the public record. Music and art were politicised to ensure a constant flow of works that extolled the virtues of the regime and its leadership. Every form of instruction, at every level of education, was rigorously policed to ensure that students were only exposed to the party and state line. Any deviation from the state's ideology exposed a person to suspicion, possible arrest and much worse. Penalties for gossip, criticism, or questioning of any aspect of the state's activities were severe in the extreme.

These episodes have inspired a genre of novels exploring the post-truth world. Arthur Koestler's *Darkness at Noon* was based on the arrest of Bukharin, a victim of the famous show trials that used wholly fabricated evidence to indict enemies of the regime. George Orwell's *1984* remains a powerful literary monument to the idea of a world in which facts of every kind are manipulated to ensure complete subordination and compliance.

Lest we imagine that this apparatus for maintaining a parallel reality belongs only to a far-flung past, we only need to turn to the testimony of Chinese and North Korean dissidents for an appropriate reminder of these techniques' currency. There is nothing at all old-fashioned or antique about trying to control reality for the larger purpose of maintaining order and stability. If this is what post-truth implies, we must acknowledge that very few democratic regimes exhibit anything like the degree of control over the truth and reality that we associate with authoritarian regimes.

This is not to say that our 'open societies' are as open as many think they are, or as open as we might like them to be. There are all manners of ways in which people try to manipulate the truth to suit their needs and interests. Indeed, the worry might be that this has become normal in advanced capitalist societies. Advertisers do it ('Washes even whiter!'), universities do it ('Amazing things happen here!'), politicians do it (Nixon: 'No event is more misunderstood than the Vietnam War'). If this is also post-truth, we must acknowledge that it is of a very different magnitude, in terms of its intensities and effects, to the efforts of authoritarian regimes to control reality and shape the lives of their citizens.

Clearly, there is a great deal at stake in controlling how we perceive the past, who is responsible for national successes and failures, how peoples and minorities are incorporated into a nation. No surprise then, to find the details are contested. These narratives are highly political and subject to being written, and rewritten, in accordance with changing priorities.

'Post-truth' or unfashionable views?

In an earlier chapter, I noted Fukuyama's description of populism as 'the label that political elites attach to policies supported by ordinary citizens that they don't like.' His point is that the concept of populism has served a useful purpose for elites, and he implies that the anger and resentment of citizens is at some level unwarranted or deluded. When we recover our senses, we'll be right back behind those mainstream parties and opinions.

Post-truth can have a similar ring. Do we think that were it not for attempts to deceive or manipulate opinion through the promotion of fake news or dodgy statistics, some citizens would not have voted for Trump or Brexit, Wilders or the AfD? Are populism and the rejection of the mainstream only possible on the basis of falsified data, lies and bullshit? The problem is the assumption that reality, or the 'facts', determine our worldviews or ideologies. It seems just as plausible to suppose that our worldview determines what we are prepared to accept as fact. The Brexit debate clearly shows what is at stake.

To the perplexity of the elites, the rubbishing of claims made by Leave campaigners has not translated into a steep decline in support for Brexit. It doesn't seem to matter that the £350 million emblazoned on the battle bus was exaggerated. It doesn't matter that the terms of the divorce from the EU are likely to be far worse than any Leave campaigner was prepared to admit, or that issues presented by the Leave campaign as easily resolvable appear deeply intractable. The data suggest that many who voted 'leave' did so less on the basis of the jumble of assorted 'facts' presented to them but more on two key issues: immigration and sovereignty. Leave voters wished to restore national sovereignty, borders and control over matters relating to the UK. Once that becomes clear, everything else makes sense. But for elites this represents turning our backs on globalisation, trans-national migration and the benefits of being part of a strong supra-national organisation. The worldview is wrong and so, therefore, must be the bedrock of assumptions that inform the worldview.

This illustrates a larger point, that we have difficulty accepting views and opinions different to our own when we are convinced of the truth and rationality of our own position. If we absolutely *know* that we are right about something, and someone contradicts this, we try to explain it by reference to their incomplete understanding of the topic, dubious grasp of the relevant facts, manipulation by others, fake news. It's a form of critique that Marxists call 'false consciousness', a view of reality at odds with the 'real' reality that lies beneath the surface of public expression. For the past half-century, the dominant ideology has insisted that open markets, trans-national migration, deregulated banking, the privatisation of public services and new public management are the best way of organising our societies. Crisis has not only punctured the financial bubble, it has also punctured the dominant *ideological* bubble. Anger and discontent have followed, encouraging the denigration of the elite worldview.

From this angle, populism looks less like the imposition of a new ideology than the return of values and opinions that seemed to have been discredited, forgotten or displaced. The consensus on 'anywhere' cosmopolitan, trans-national values and beliefs is challenged by the return of 'somewhere' nativist beliefs that focus on restoring a sense of common identity and culture. But, as many have commented, if populism – particularly in its right-wing nativist guise – is anything, it is a moment of nostalgia for a lost world, for its lost understandings and its bygone sense of how the world functions, and for whom. Perhaps the spark for populism is less post-truth and more 'alter-truth', a set of values, beliefs and principles at odds with elite and mainstream views. To invoke Fukuyama, could it be that what we ascribe to the operation of post-truth is really the resurfacing, or re-emergence, of views that elites don't like and need to explain away by reference to some underhand process?

Don't want more migrants in our societies? Must be because we have been lied to about the advantages of a multicultural, diverse society. Don't believe in the benefits of open markets and privatisation? Must be because we misunderstand the benefits of trickle-down economics and capitalist competition. Don't think that membership of supra-national bodies is in our interest? Must be because we have been hoodwinked into thinking that the costs outweigh the benefits of membership.

Conclusion

Concern about the impact of lies, deceit and manipulation on politics is widespread. Many want to attribute the extraordinary events witnessed in democratic societies over the past few years to post-truth. We have an abnormal politics because an abnormal relationship is developing between reality and truth. Democracy, it is held, requires openness, transparency and integrity. The development of post-truth rubs against these values, with unwelcome results.

Compelling though this might sound, we must be cautious in deriving conclusions of this kind. Whilst the concept of post-truth might be new, many precedents suggest it is the means – digital software and the Internet – that are new, not the ends. Lying, deceit and manipulation, if not constants in political life, are certainly familiar themes, stretching back to the dawn of democracy in ancient Athens. The twentieth century saw the emergence of regimes that perfected the art of fabricating evidence according to their own needs.

This doesn't mean these developments are of no consequence, and we should be sanguine about fake news, data manipulation and all the rest. What is becoming clear is that the Internet, and many of its more popular platforms, such as Facebook, offer a panoply of new tools and devices for manipulating and harvesting data for nefarious political purposes. The Cambridge Analytica scandal of 2018 is a stark warning of this reality.

The problem, as ever, is establishing causal links between these developments and political outcomes. Was the election of Trump *primarily* due to fake news, the manipulation of data by organisations such as Cambridge Analytica, and more generally by his cavalier disregard for the truth in pursuit of his political cause? Was the outcome of the Brexit referendum due to a small group of clever people hoodwinking the British public with their promises of extra funding for the health service? Is the emergence of the far right on continental Europe due to the manipulation of people's perception of Islam, or the propagation of false information concerning the exact number of refugees arriving from the Middle East?

No doubt some of this has an impact. Exaggerating statistics, inflating claims, playing on people's fears through negative advertising undoubtedly works. If it didn't, politicians wouldn't waste their money on these techniques, and nor would advertisers. It's why left and right, both mainstream and populist, use them. Every side tries to squeeze as much value out of playing with facts, manipulating data, putting the best possible gloss on themselves and their policies that they can, given the resources they have. It's what the term 'spin' was invented to describe.

It would be wrong to dismiss the concerns of those who see a connection between manipulation of data and political outcomes. Some of this helps us to understand the emergence of populist parties and movements. People have undoubtedly been nudged into accepting positions and policies that they might not otherwise have supported, or about which they might have been more ambivalent. But it takes more than a nudge from a poster, some fiery oratory, a bus passing by with a fanciful number written on it to get people to sign up for outsider and anti-establishment views.

Without a sense that elites have let citizens down, none of this is likely to make enough of a difference; the kind of difference that shifts outcomes away from the mainstream and towards outsiders. Crisis generates an appetite for something new, something different, something immediate. It makes people receptive to ideas and positions that might otherwise seem eccentric or unacceptable. Amidst distrust and scepticism of the mainstream we become more receptive to radical solutions, oddball leaders, extreme or heterodox policies. But it wasn't data manipulation that generated a sense of crisis amongst the electorates of many democracies. Post-truth didn't create recession, austerity or the collapse of trust in the political class. For a growing number of citizens, the elites are responsible for the problems that confront us. This is why parties and movements critical of elites have gained traction, notwithstanding the dominance of their world-view, their values and indeed their 'facts'.

6

Conclusion – what is to be done about populism?

Populism is widely regarded as one of the key threats of our time. Newspapers, particularly since the events of 2016, have been full of alarming pieces seeking to understand the populist threat and what can be done about it. Fear makes for excellent copy – that should not be forgotten – but even so, most commentators recognise that populism raises legitimate concerns. Populism is a departure from 'normal' or mainstream politics, and that can be unsettling. It's also a politics that might usher in extreme or radical policies that affect people in various ways. At the time of writing, this is particularly the case for those on the receiving end of nativist policies in Europe and North America.

In the USA, Trump has indicated that he wants to remove immigrants who have arrived without permits, 'dreamers' (young people who arrived illegally as children), and those whose status might be doubtful. He has made life uncomfortable for Muslims, or people with relatives from countries he has identified as a threat; the ban on travellers from specific countries has widely been seen as a Muslim ban. He has belittled 'shithole' countries, making recent arrivals from these areas wonder if they will be sent back because they are less desirable than white middle-class North Europeans. In France, six million citizens of North African heritage contemplate what their fate will be if Marine Le Pen wins power at the next presidential election. Similar sentiments are shared by Muslims in Holland, refugees in Italy, new arrivals in countries such as Austria, Hungary and Poland. In the UK, many millions of EU citizens remain unsure of their status when Brexit finally happens.

More generally, many wonder what life will be like in democracies dominated by self-proclaimed 'outsiders', who might not feel the same sense of affinity with democratic institutions and processes as the mainstream parties who have dominated the political scene for so long. Concern mixes with trepidation, as the true colours of anti-establishment figures become known. Perhaps they won't be as bad as they seem. Perhaps their bark will be worse than their bite. Perhaps they will be tamed or controlled by the force of financial markets, by public opinion or by international institutions. In the absence of many examples of populists gaining power in the advanced democracies, speculation is rife about what this transition from parties of protest to parties of government foretells.

Such speculation also concerns the nature of the democratic system itself and how robust it will prove if taken over by outsiders, radicals and self-proclaimed anti-establishment movements. Are the institutions and processes so well implanted that they will resist becoming the playthings of demagogues and despots? Will the state resist attempts to make it an instrument for a new form of governance?

These questions divide experts. In the months after Trump's election, debate centred on the nature of what is termed 'the deep state', the layers of officialdom of the military and intelligence communities, lying far beneath the immediate oversight and control of the President and Congress. What kind of autonomy do they have? Might they be able to derail or undermine a president for whom they had no sympathy or who seemed to threaten their position or privileges? This is not a new theme.

There has long been speculation about the relative autonomy of the state, and in particular the intelligence community, from politicians and the governing institutions. It's a genre well explored in popular culture through films and novels such as *A Very British Coup*, which explores the reaction of the British deep state to the election of a Labour Party leader with an uncanny resemblance to Jeremy Corbyn (spoiler alert: it doesn't end well). The question becomes particularly pertinent in an era when populism might become more widespread and achieve longevity, as opposed to being just a flash in the pan as it can sometimes appear. Will the state come to the defence of democratic values, or roll over and meekly accept illiberal and potentially fascistic regimes?

No matter one's view of the nature of populism, it must be recognised that many people fear it, and that much of this fear seems well-grounded. What is to be done? How should we think about responding to populism? How should citizens safeguard themselves and their communities from the 'populist upsurge'?

To answer this question satisfactorily, it's essential for us to fix on what is distinctive about populism, as opposed to other kinds of political regime or movement, such as authoritarianism, fascism or nationalism. What has become obvious is that *populism is a form of political discourse in which 'the people' stand in an antagonistic relationship to the elites*. From this, most of the other features that are associated with populism follow: the idea of populist parties and movements as 'outsiders', as anti-establishment, and as against the status quo. It also confirms the idea of populism as, in some sense, a threat. As the people are set against the governing class, they are told there must be a radical break with the present to save them or put them back in the position they would have been in were it not for the actions of elites. These themes have been constant throughout this discussion. This definition permits us to highlight what is distinctively populist about parties and movements. Equally, it helps us to clarify what populism is not.

Invoking 'the people' is not populist

Populism refers to a relationship between the people on the one hand and the elites on the other. Identifying the people as the subject of politics is not itself populism. The people is the *demos* and the *demos* is the subject of a democratic politics.

The idea that we can identify populist politics by identifying the people in the discourse of parties and leaders doesn't help clarify what is distinctive about populism. Reference to the people is pronounced in populist rhetoric, because populism arises where the perception that there is a schism or antagonism between the people and the elites arises. But a form of discourse or demands framed simply in terms of what 'the people' need or want is not itself populist; it's how politics operates under democratic conditions. The American Constitution opens with the famous line, 'We the People of the United States'; this evocation of the people is not populist. Most constitutions include reference to the people, because when a democratic political system is being established it is entirely appropriate to reference 'the people' as the entity for whom the constitution is brought into being. The same goes for national anthems and other artefacts seeking to develop and speak to a sense that the people, the subject of democracy, is unified in what it desires, in this case the founding of a new state.

Moving to everyday political discourse, claiming to speak on behalf of 'the people' is often cited as a populist move. But, in a democracy, there's nothing unusual or untoward in talking about what the people want or need. For politicians, the aim is to make their message chime with as many voters as possible: 'I know that the people want more public services', 'I understand that people don't always agree with a rise in taxation', and so on. This is the *lingua franca* of democracies. Politicians reach out to as many citizens as possible in the hope of increasing their popularity and their chances at the next election.

What marks the populist from other kinds of politician is the emphatic distinction between what the people want on the one hand and what is being supplied by elites, the political system or the establishment on the other. The objective is to show how the needs and interests of the people are being ignored by the elites, and thus that the people should be looking beyond or outside the governing class for leadership. It demonstrates that there is an antagonism between the people and the governing class, and implies that the antagonism can only be overcome by installing someone who understands what the people really want and need. Hence the dynamic behind the populist interlocutor who claims to understand the people, and to do so from outside or beyond the elites: 'Follow me, I can save you from them.' The fact that leaders such as Farage and Le Pen are themselves from the upper reaches of society, and part of what many citizens would understand as the elite, is irrelevant. The framing of the discourse is what counts, and the nature of the claims about the political context.

Why does this matter? We often hear that citizens are being 'turned off' politics because of the negativity and the antagonism that characterises politics under democratic conditions. Politics can feel like a battleground. Fractious debates in parliaments and on television, Twitter wars, claim and counterclaim, accentuate the apparently oppositional nature of politics under democratic conditions: 'Don't believe him, believe me.' One of the more commented-on features of populism is the way populist leaders seek to rise above the fray in search of a unifying posture designed to distance themselves from the unedifying hurly-burly of the background. Positioning oneself as someone seeking to unify the people rather than divide them, as seeking to rise above ideology, party politics and the usual paraphernalia of democratic politics, has proved a useful strategy for building a popular base.

The emergence of a strong figure who claims they have all the answers, and who thus seems indifferent to others' views or opinions, is an alarming prospect. We ought therefore to be worrying about the emergence of political leaders who position themselves beyond the usual antagonisms and portray themselves as saviours of the people. One cannot be outside or beyond the pluralistic struggles that define democratic contestation. To say one can be sets one in opposition to an important feature that differentiates democracy from other kinds of political system.

This seems compelling, but the danger is in confusing the rhetorical strategies used by politicians with policy recommendations. Portraying themselves as 'above the fray', as 'beyond ideology', 'on the side of the people' has paid dividends for generations of presidential and prime ministerial hopefuls. More than this, it is essential for the successful prosecution of the role. As the political theorist Pierre Rosanvallon explains, in a democracy there is always a balancing act between an appeal to what he terms 'particularity' on the one hand and 'generality' on the other. Democracy is composed of a multitude of shifting identities and interests, of different groups with different agendas. These are the different particularities that we find in a complex modern setting. However, democracy also requires that someone speaks for the people, for the generality, especially during times of strife or crisis but more generally to speak for the public interest. Democracy means rule by the people, but since for practical reasons we cannot rule ourselves, we need someone to do it for us. Since the people cannot speak for itself, someone must speak for it. It's therefore quite unexceptional for us to expect the president or the prime minister to fulfil that role. This is why those who want to occupy national office need to look like and sound like a representative of the people.

If we think that a rhetoric framed in governing in the name of the people represents a threat to the people, we're in danger of losing touch with how political discourse functions in a democracy, and how successful politicians position themselves in relation to the generality. Successful presidents and prime ministers can make the demanding transition from sounding as if they're only interested in one section of the population to sounding as if they care about the people, the generality. In the absence of a discourse that resonates with the people, we tend to see a disruptive style of politics emerging.

What does this disruption look like in practice? To take an example, Belgium was recently thrown into political hiatus by the deep divisions in its society. Belgium has two main ethnic groups, one Flemish-speaking and the other French-speaking. Elections over the last few decades have seen pro-Flemish parties elected and the French-speaking populace querying the result. The fear is that a Flemish party will rule in the interests of the dominant ethnicity, as opposed to doing what is best for the whole Belgian people. Demands flow to rerun the election, to establish minority rights in the constitution or devolve powers to regional government to ensure that the minority is not disadvantaged. These demands are signs that the needs and interests of 'the people' are threatened because of the domination of a specific group or ethnicity. Democracy, by contrast, requires that those needs be set to one side in the interests of the generality and not the particularity such as a dominant ethnic group.

Speaking in the name of the people, governing in the name of the people, invoking the people as the subject of politics should not be regarded as populist, even incipiently. A *democratic* politics, as opposed to a politics based on identity, ethnicity or particularity, is framed in rhetorical terms. If we insist that speaking in the name of the people is characteristic of populism, the implication is that politicians should speak only for their own constituencies and supporter base and forget about the needs and interests of the people. Surely, the opposite is true: those interested in protecting and promoting democracy must insist that those who want to represent the generality say what they will do in the needs and interests of the people, as opposed to the particular groups, identities or special interests that might have supported them, and with which they might otherwise be identified. In short, we should not be abandoning the idea of democracy as rule by the people for fear that this will make our politics more populist.

Populism is not a variety of far-right politics

Populism is often equated with extreme or far-right politics. Indeed, it can sometimes seem that 'populism' and 'the far right' are interchangeable expressions. It is certainly true there is no shortage of far-right leaders who are also populist, including the Le Pens, Orbán, Wilders and Jörg Haider, former leader of the Austrian Freedom Party (FPÖ). But numerous figures on the left are also labelled populist, from the leaders of *Podemos* and *Syriza* to radical leftists such as Bernie Sanders, Jean-Luc Mélanchon and Jeremy Corbyn. More recently, Emmanuel Macron has been described as a populist, of a centrist or liberal kind. Beppe Grillo's M5S is also usually regarded as populist, notwithstanding that it combines elements of right-wing and left-wing ideology with eccentric contributions from environmentalism, deliberative democracy, cyber-Utopianism and others. Let's also not forget that the very first example of populism is usually regarded as being the Russian *Narodniks*, who were a variety of romantic agrarian communists.

How do we fit this kaleidoscope into the equating of populism with the far right? We can draw one of two conclusions. Either the left-wing and centrist figures can be regarded as so similar to right-wing ones that they can be treated the same for the purpose of political analysis, or the left-wing figures and parties are of such minor significance in the overall story of populism that they can be disregarded as outliers.

Neither conclusion is particularly convincing. As critics of the concept of totalitarianism have long argued, if we disregard ideology, we end up with a conservative form of analysis which implies that all radical political initiatives are incipiently authoritarian, because they share certain traits and characteristics, even though their objectives might be very different. This claim might be effective in ideological terms, as a 'red scare', a means to wean citizens away from radical movements and parties, but it's less satisfactory for comparative political analysis.

The second conclusion has a somewhat ironic air, given that the early history of populism was about left-wing movements and parties. Even before we come to recent cases such as Iglesias and Tsipras, the *Narodniks* were populist, in nearly everyone's reading; Huey Long was a New Deal Democrat; many of the *caudillo* in Latin America were also on the left. The idea that we should disregard examples such as these in favour of an interpretation of populism as a right-wing phenomenon is out of touch with contemporary reality, as well as historical antecedent. It should also make us wonder why we need a term such as populism: if populism is of the far right and the far right can be equated with populism, it's not easy to see what function the concept serves.

What's going on? What appears to be happening is that commentators are concerned about how invoking the people creates an in group–out group dynamic which, when allied to a nativist rhetoric, provides the basis for a politics of scapegoating groups: migrants, minorities and so on. This is indeed how far-right politics tends to work; the in group is often defined in terms of racial, ethnic or religious characteristics, implying that if you don't share these characteristics you are not part of the people. But invoking the people need not necessarily lead to an in–out dynamic. In democratic discourse, 'the people' is used more generally to signify everyone in a particular political community, irrespective of their ethnicity or other characteristics. 'We the People' is not, in this sense, exclusionary or populist. It's a way of asserting a common purpose and identity based on equal citizenship in a given territory. This is how discourse under democratic conditions works, by appealing to the people as the subject of politics. This is not a right-wing or a left-wing gesture; it is a gesture with no ideological inflection. Therefore, we hear both right-wing and left-wing parties claiming to speak for the people.

If populism is not a variety of far-right politics, might it still be true that most far-right politics is a variety of populism? Might it be that we are discussing a concept that has acquired strong authoritarian and nativist overtones because of the preponderance of far-right parties and movements?

This is a more compelling explanation. It implies that far-right ideology has a natural affinity with populism, which might not be the case with left-wing or liberal politics. However, the affinity is not 'natural' but an effect of how far-right and nativist views have set themselves on a collision course with the dominant ideology of most advanced democracies, the 'anywhere' sensibility that welcomes globalisation and ever-increasing flows of people, capital and goods. This sensibility underpins the idea of the European single market, where any citizen of an EU country can move, without impediment, to any other EU country. It insists, with Angela Merkel, that we have obligations to others to look after refugees, promote human rights and play our part as good international citizens.

The issue is that elite values point in one direction, whereas the values and instincts of many citizens seem to point in another. This collision of value systems translates into a populist rhetoric of a nativist kind, in which elites are accused of being out of touch. But the key point is that it is nativist values that are driving the populist rhetoric. Nativism finds itself in antagonism to the cosmopolitan values of the elites, leading to the call for leadership from outside those elites.

Lest we overlook it, a different antagonism arises in relation to the neo-liberal side of the 'neo-liberal globalisation' ideology. Left-wing parties and movements also find themselves in antagonism with elites, due to the elites' adoption of austerity policies in the wake of the global financial crisis and recession. *Podemos*, *Syriza*, Sanders and Corbyn can be considered populists, not because left-wing ideology is inherently populist, but because at this particular moment left-wing ideals and values are in sharp contradiction to the policy direction pursued by most governments.

The fact that most far-right political parties and movements have a populist element in their discourse should not obscure the fact that many left-wing parties and movements can also appear populist in current conditions. Since both are critical of the current stance of elites, albeit for quite different reasons, they both adopt a rhetoric in which the people are said to be in antagonism to the political class and establishment. The perhaps greater success of the far right in recent elections doesn't make populism a far-right phenomenon. It just means that for the present we can call on more examples of populism from the right than we can from the left.

Populism is not an ideology

Assuming that by 'ideology' we mean a belief system or worldview that offers a sense of how we should organise our societies, populism is not an ideology. There are few texts or writings to indicate what anyone calling themselves populist means by a populist society. We lack a coherent or consistent intellectual lineage, of the kind that generally characterises ideologies, whether of the left or the right. The one key feature that nearly everyone agrees characterises populism, reference to an antagonism between the people and the elites, indicates little about what lies ahead, what kind of society we should construct or how we should overcome that antagonism to give the people what they need or want.

Populists do not all need to possess the *same* values or belief system to make them populists. The elite's values and belief system can be challenged from different angles. Socialists, and those on the left, reject the dominant ideology of recent decades, neo-liberal globalisation and its focus on the market and privatisation. Those on the right oppose open borders and the free movement of people. Green parties oppose the lack of concern for the planet shown by people's unsustainable lifestyles. There are multiple ways in which we can take issue with dominant values; each of those ways can translate into a form of discourse in which the issue is less about the policies or approach of one party or leader and more about the underpinning values and beliefs of the elites or the system in general.

Why does this matter? Understanding that populism is not an ideology matters in terms of rescuing populism, as a concept, from those who want, paradoxically, to use it as a weapon of ideological combat, that is to promote a view of oppositional politics as authoritarian and undemocratic. While plenty of authoritarians use populist discourse to advance their cause, it is not the *populism* that threatens the integrity of democratic systems but the authoritarianism, the insistence on subordinating individual preference to uniformity of outlook and behaviour. There are forms of oppositional politics that move the other way, insisting the problem with contemporary democratic politics is that it is not democratic enough; it fails to engage citizens or provide opportunities for meaningful participation. It is held captive by the elites, with the result that pluralism has become notional rather than real, the ideological cover for plutocracy, of government of, by and for the wealthy.

In recent years the number of left-wing movements espousing an anti-elitist line, from Occupy to #15M to *Nuit debout* (the popular movement that swept France in 2017 protesting against new labour laws), has been on the rise. Although these movements do not identify themselves as populist (barely any do), Occupy's claim that it represents the 99% is a classic populist gesture. These are oppositional movements of a populist type as far as their discourse and rhetoric are concerned. They are not immune to authoritarian tendencies but, by and large, they seek to provide a non-dogmatic, non-programmatic style of politics of a 'prefigurative' kind, highlighting the gap between how democracy works under contemporary conditions and how it *might* work once the people are freed from plutocratic control.

If populism is not an ideology in the usual sense of a belief system or worldview, could it nevertheless be regarded as an ideology in some other way? Could, as some suggest, populism be a 'weak' ideology comprising certain themes: centrality of the people, a critique of elites and a belief in the superiority of strong leadership in the name of the 'general will'?

The 'general will' has a handy association with a kind of authoritarianism masquerading as democracy. It's for this reason that some see it as a meaningful trope for exploring populism as a kind of pseudo-democratic impulse. It was popularised by Rousseau, who has often been accused of being a 'proto-totalitarian', for his suggestion that majoritarianism be subordinated to the general will. But Rousseau was merely grappling with the puzzle described by Rosanvallon; that in a democracy someone, or something, has to represent the generality: the common good, the public interest, the general will. Rousseau might not have landed on a satisfactory or appropriate mechanism for resolving the issue of how one establishes the generality but his view that in a democracy the law should express the will of the community is normally regarded as uncontroversial.

The idea of populism as a 'weak' ideology encapsulating certain themes doesn't appear to get us any closer to understanding its particular dynamic. Whether a party or a movement finds itself in opposition to elites is a matter of whether its ideology, which might be leftist, rightist or centrist, brings it into opposition to the beliefs and values of the elites. Nativists oppose elites because they're against cosmopolitanism, liberal humanitarianism and trans-nationalism. Left populists, such as *Podemos*, oppose the elites in Spain, because in their view the country has been plagued by a generation of neo-liberal politicians, *la casta*, which has been acting in concert to undermine welfare policies while enriching themselves and their client groups. Neither oppose elites because of a shared attachment to the idea of the 'general will', but because they are opposed to what the elites are doing to undermine the values and principles for which they stand.

Whatever contortions are applied to the concept of ideology, populism fails the test. It is not a worldview, a belief system, a set of values. It isn't even a 'weak' consensus on certain themes, which we should be suspicious of. The link between the groups, parties and movements I have discussed is not ideological but political. It arises from the sense that the elites are not acting in the best interests of the people and have to be replaced by someone, or some party, that will. Given the multitude of reasons why a person might have an animus against the elites, it hardly advances the analysis to describe this in terms of an *ideology*, particularly when the opposing elites do so from radically different starting points and with different objectives. Surely a better way of framing it is to turn the matter around and note that one of the chief causes of the multiplying populisms we see around us is the faltering hegemony of the elite ideology – neo-liberal globalisation – that has held sway for the past three or four decades. This allows us to see that what is at stake in the discussion is not so much any threat posed to democracy by populism, more the inability of the governing elites to stave off growing scepticism about their ability to rule in the name of the people.

Populism is not anti-democratic

Populism is widely regarded as anti-democratic. The media is full of alarm about the continuing advance of populist parties and movements; about the populist threat. There *are* populist movements and parties that pose a threat to democracy, but they do so because of their authoritarian policies and sectarian approach to governing, not because they are populist. There are populist groups and parties who are not authoritarian. Indeed, there are populist movements that seek the expansion of democracy to include greater engagement and participation by citizens. So how has populism come to be seen as a threat to democracy?

The answer lies with the conflation of the attack on 'elites', which is core to populist discourse, with the attack on 'democratic institutions and practices', which is not. Saying that I don't trust those who hold power to do what is best for the people is not the same as saying that I don't trust democratic institutions and processes. Far from it. My position might be that whilst I completely support democracy, I think that those in charge are corrupt, incompetent or out to fill their own pockets. With a different group of politicians or representatives, we might find that things get a lot better.

If this analysis sounds a little stretched, we need to note that, notwithstanding the upsurge of outsider and anti-establishment parties, faith in democracy and democratic institutions remains largely intact, according to authoritative surveys such as the Eurobarometer. Citizens are quite capable of distinguishing between the elites who happen to be in charge and the democratic institutions and processes that may be threatened by those same elites. They can distinguish between the governing class and the mechanisms of governance. What we find, increasingly, is that citizens are becoming more disillusioned with the political class, and are becoming 'uncoupled' from them. The differences between mainstream parties that once seemed so important are becoming less so as we detect fewer differences between them. The similarities begin to outweigh the differences, giving citizens the impression of a class of politicians, the elites, who, many people feel, are in it for themselves. We might regret such a stance, and feel it to be an unrealistic expression of 'anti-politics', but it's surely not an *undemocratic* sentiment. On the contrary, it might be a manifestation of a desire to make democratic politics more meaningful, more participatory and more engaging.

If this is true for citizens, why could it not be true for political parties and movements? Why do we find it difficult to imagine that a critique of elites, of the governing class, might be offered in the name of improving or renewing democracy, as opposed to undermining it? There are a variety of reasons, and I have covered some of them. It might be because commentators feel that an appeal to the people is an inherently authoritarian gesture. It might be because of the association between the people and a nation, or homogenous entity. It might be because some populist leaders and parties that have come to power have shown authoritarian tendencies.

Populism offers a critique of the behaviour, ideology or comportment of elites and the governing class, which does not necessarily imply a critique of democratic institutions and practices. On the contrary, a critique of this kind may stem from the feeling that the behaviour or ideology of existing elites is itself detrimental to democracy and thus, only by challenging them are we likely to be able to promote and renew democracy. When, for example, the eminent political scientist Peter Mair offers the view that our democracies are marked by a void that should be filled with discussion, deliberation and engagement, he offers an analysis of the kind that underpins the left populist critique of contemporary democracy, and even some right-wing variants, such as the Leave voters motivated by the desire to repatriate powers back to the UK from the 'bureaucratic' EU.

The point Mair and other specialists make is that the governing class as a whole is complicit in the denuding of democracy, through tacit acceptance of a dominant ideology that brooks little criticism or argument. This has resulted in a collapse of faith in the ability of citizens to influence, let alone direct, their lives in the manner we expect in a democracy, which, to recall Lincoln, is supposed to mean government 'of the people, by the people, for the people'. If democracy has become captive to cartels, parties, plutocrats and special interests, as Mair claims, it stands to reason that the way to disrupt the pattern is to develop and build on a critique of elite behaviour 'in the name of the people'. Rather than threatening democracy, populism may be a way of revitalising it.

Populism does not threaten pluralism

A variant of the argument that populism is undemocratic is rehearsed in several texts that have been published since Trump's election and the continued expansion of illiberal political forces throughout central and eastern Europe. The argument is that populism is against pluralism, and by extension liberalism, without which liberal democracy cannot be sustained.

The nature and form of our democracy has been shaped, in large measure, by the need to recognise and indeed celebrate differences by encouraging freedom of speech and open competitive elections between individual candidates, as well as between political parties that seek to aggregate opinions and preferences and represent them in the system of government. It's a system and a culture that has proved remarkably resilient for two centuries at least and yet many commentators deem it to be under grave threat from the rise of populism.

The threat arises because of the populist insistence that 'the people' be regarded as a homogenous entity possessing certain characteristics, needs and interests, which it is the leader's or the party's task to represent. Normally, in a democracy, we establish what these needs and interests are by directly asking citizens which party or candidate they feel best represents their views and opinions. Accepting that the response will be plural, given the complexity of modern settings, we accept that we need a plurality of candidates and parties in order to represent fully the various positions that citizens will hold. The same is not apparently true for populist leaders and parties. Because populism sees the people as a homogenous entity, that is, as an entity characterised by a fundamental similarity of ethnicity, culture and worldview, the pluralism of the democrats is illusory, superfluous or unnecessary. What we should be doing is governing in the interest of the people as a singular undifferentiated subject, not a plurality of subjects.

This should alert us to the perils lurking in the populists' siren call to the people. And there is plenty of evidence to back up the analysis. Many of those regularly labelled as populists do indeed have a narrow view of how we should interpret the needs and interests of the people. Particularly on the right, 'the people' has a strong ethnic and cultural connotation, implying that those who don't share an ethnicity should be excluded from consideration. Nativism trades on the understanding that when we are talking about 'what the people want', we implicitly understand that this refers to 'what the dominant ethnicity or identity wants'. But deploying the concept of the people to indicate definite traits or characteristics doesn't rule out using it in an open and inclusive manner, as in the US Constitution, where 'the people' refers to everyone in a given political community.

How has 'the people' come to be exclusive rather than inclusive? Here, we come back to the issue that seems to underpin the critique of populism: fear of generality and invoking the *demos* as the subject of politics. 'The people' is, for some tastes, too emotive a term. It invokes the 'general will' of subservience to the totality. We're not supposed to speak on behalf of others ('Not in my name!'), let alone something as grand and abstract as 'the people'. We're supposed to tiptoe round the issue, by emphasising where possible the myriad ways in which we differ from each other: colour of skin, ethnicity, background, class, sex, gender, nationality and so on. With all these differences in mind, how could it not be at least incipiently totalitarian to erase all this 'in the name of the people'?

The point of the populist position is to invoke the people in opposition to the elites. Populism is, in this sense, different from nativism or other variants of nationalism, because it rotates around the nature of a specific antagonism (people vs elites) that is political, not ethnic or national, in character. This is not to say that nativism cannot be populist. It can, as Le Pen, Wilders and the broad swathe of European nativist movements show. But populism is not the same as nativism or nationalism. They specify who 'the people' are in terms of definite ethnic and cultural characteristics, but populism describes an antagonism between elites and the people, irrespective of any characteristics they are said to possess. Populism becomes nativist or nationalistic in character when this antagonism is conjoined to an idea about the ethnicity, religion or nationality of the people in question. If I say the people have been let down by the elites, that is not a nativist sentiment. But if I add that elites have let down white Australians, I've added a component that underpins a very particular kind of populism: national or nativist populism.

For populism, there is only one sense in which the people are seen in terms of a 'homogenous' group and that is the sense of being members of a particular political community. Everything else is left open. By extension, populism itself does not close or threaten pluralism merely by invoking 'the people'. On the contrary, populism can arise when the desired pluralism of the democratic order is thought to be threatened by the actions of the elites. The populism of Occupy ('We are the 99%'), #15M, *Nuit debout* and so on is not a call to shut down pluralism. It is not a call for the defence of a homogenous entity, a specific identity or particular ethnicity. Rather, the point is to identify the elite, the 1%, whose wealth and privilege permits them, so critics argue, to control public debate and discourage the open engagement and participation that should characterise a healthy, functioning democracy. Populism is here used as a tool to reinvigorate the case for pluralism against a proportionately much smaller grouping, the very wealthy. It is a populism in the name of the people but also in the name of pluralism. It's a populism that argues for opening the public sphere to minority voices and views and which desires meaningful political contestation, not a system in which wealth and privilege determine key political outcomes.

Populism is not the cause of the crisis

The broad consensus amongst political scientists and expert commentators is that our democracies are in crisis. Bookshop tables groan under the weight of texts devoted to the issue: *The Life and Death of Democracy* by John Keane, *Why we Hate Politics* by Colin Hay, *Post-Democracy* by Colin Crouch, *Can Democracy be Saved?* by Donatella della Porta, *Ruling the Void* by Peter Mair, *Defending Politics* by Matthew Flinders; just a few of the better-known works exploring the contours of the issue.

Much of the blame seems to be placed at populism's door. Populists stir up trouble. They find divisions in populations that, until recently, seemed tolerant and respectful. They luxuriate in berating those in power without demonstrating any competence or ability to themselves govern a complex society. They offer simple solutions to complex issues that actually require give and take, negotiation and an iterative approach to policymaking. In short, populism is an unwelcome distraction for societies grappling with a range of urgent issues requiring mature reflection and debate, such as climate change, automation, migration and more.

We are left with the image of populism as a cause of the ills afflicting democracy. But this is to get cause and effect the wrong way around. The clue lies in some of the books I mentioned at the start of this section. Most were written well before the current 'explosion' of populism; some barely touch on the emergence of far-right parties and movements in countries such as France, Holland and Hungary over the past couple of decades. Rather, they take their cue from the markers we use to measure the health of democracy, which have been declining since the 1960s. Voter turnout, membership of political parties, trust in politicians and interest in mainstream electoral politics – all have been falling for the past half-century.

The better-known explanations for this decline barely touch on populism. They include the view that citizens have become more 'critical', with the result that they are more sceptical about the claims and promises of politicians and perhaps less inclined to engage with mainstream politics (Pippa Norris). Others (such as Colin Hay) dwell on the domination of a worldview that insists on prioritising the market over the public sphere, with the result that citizens are turned off by politics, while yet others (such as Zygmunt Bauman) suspect that long-range sociological changes mean we have less time and less inclination to engage with matters of collective interest as opposed to issues that directly relate to us individually. I could go on. The point is that the crisis of democracy predates the current populist upsurge. When specialists look for causes of this crisis, they rarely invoke the upsurge of outsider or anti-establishment political forces. Little surprise; until recently many of these forces were either very marginal or had not yet made their appearance.

Populism is not a cause of the current crisis; it is an effect of it. It arises when 'normal politics', the familiar politics characterised by a pendulum movement between centre left and centre right, breaks down and citizens begin to look outside the mainstream for solutions to the issues that concern them. It arises when citizens begin to feel that the differences between mainstream political forces, which might once have seemed so marked, are less significant than what unites them.

Nonetheless we might want to say that populism doesn't help us address the causes of the crisis, and so contributes to it. I might not have caused the fire in my neighbour's house but if I throw a can of petrol on the blaze, I make matters worse, not better. Might not something similar be said about populism? We can accept both that populism didn't create the current crisis and insist that, with its divisive rhetoric and simple solutions, it is unlikely to make matters better, and indeed, will probably make them worse.

Many people will, no doubt, sympathise with this assessment, given the hiatus unleashed in the wake of recent political developments in the USA, UK, Italy and elsewhere. However, populism doesn't offer a consistent prescription for the ills confronting society, in the manner of classic ideologies such as socialism and liberalism. Rather, the appearance of populism tells us something important about the dynamic at work in a society: citizens are beginning to lose faith in the political class and its ability to act in the best interests of society. For this reason they are, in increasing numbers, willing to trust outsiders or anti-establishment parties to resolve the crisis and steer us in the direction of a better society.

In a crisis-afflicted society, a range of outsider groups and parties will have different analyses of what is going wrong and what should be done to rectify it. In the USA, for example, we were close to a situation in which Bernie Sanders might have faced Donald Trump. Both are, at one level, populists but their analysis of what is going wrong in the USA and how to fix it are quite different. In the run-off for the French presidential election in 2017, Marine Le Pen came up against Emmanuel Macron. Both claimed, with varying legitimacy, to be outsiders, yet their political programmes, as well as their reading of the state of play in France, were different. In the Italian general election of 2018, the top two parties in the popular vote were Beppe Grillo's M5S and Matteo Salvini's *Lega*; both populist but with quite different political stances. The resulting stand-off lasted several weeks, as they sought to thrash out a position they could both accept without the proposed alliance immediately falling apart. Sanders, Macron, Grillo: all very different, all populists in their own fashion. All outsiders. All with their own reading of what's going wrong in their societies and what needs to be done to get them back on their feet.

Given the variety of ways in which populism can express itself – right-wing, left-wing, centrist – do we really want to say that no matter in which form it appears, populism is bound to make the situation worse? This might make sense if, for example, we think all populisms are authoritarian, all require a dictatorial figurehead or that pluralism was bound to suffer. But none of these elements are essential to understanding populism. There are non-authoritarian populisms. There are populisms that don't have obvious leaders, charismatic or otherwise. And there are populisms that arise to defend pluralism against the forces and impulses that seem to threaten it.

I am not claiming that populist parties and movements are always constructive, positive contributors to the renewal of democracy. Plainly, there are populist figures and movements that are anything but. Rather, I am claiming that populism is not necessarily detrimental to democracy. In certain circumstances it can be *a* means, perhaps *the* means, to address some of the deeper-rooted and more chronic issues that contribute to the sense of democracy being in crisis. In short, populism did not cause the current hiatus we are witnessing in our democracies; it's one of its effects. Whether populism can help or hinder the renewal of democracy, whether it can address some of the root causes of the crisis, depends on the analysis that a given group or party offers, as well as the efficacy of the measures it proposes to address citizens' fears, concerns and insecurities.

What *is* to be done about populism?

Notwithstanding this set of contrarian responses, we must acknowledge that the issues and concerns many people have about the current direction of politics are real and should not be waved away as misguided or without foundation. The issue is not whether Le Pen, Trump or Orbán, and what they stand for, is any less concerning now than when we started this discussion. It is whether we've clarified the nature of the threat, or confused matters by weaving together different kinds of threat with different kinds of cause. Mention of these three figures is useful in this respect. They are all populists, according to most of the commentary, and they are all authoritarians. However, populism is not authoritarianism; it is important to keep them apart so that we can see what is at stake in terms of thinking about how to respond to contemporary developments.

Imagine a Venn diagram of two circles; one area labelled 'populism' and the other labelled 'authoritarianism'. Where the two intersect, we find 'authoritarian-populism'. To one side is non-authoritarian populism, which could complement existing forms of representative democracy, or even enhance them. To the other is non-populist authoritarianism, forms of authoritarianism that are not constituted in populist terms but rather in terms of the necessity or desirability that a certain kind of elite governs in the name of society. There is continuing debate, for example, about whether Orbán can really be identified as a populist. On the one hand, he has won multiple elections and presents himself as being in favour of stability against the swirling uncertainty that confronts the Hungarian people as they face a refugee crisis and security concerns to the east. On the other hand, he is critical of the EU establishment and draws much of his popularity from his anti-Brussels, anti-cosmopolitan outlook. Does this make him populist?

Many of the fears and worries about populism that we have been rehearsing concern the intersecting area, authoritarian populism. Various competing definitions of populism search for its roots, or its inner logic. Populism is certainly amenable to authoritarianism. But as the Venn diagram suggests, this may be only part of the picture. We also need to be aware that there are forms of populism that are not authoritarian; indeed, might be expressly anti-authoritarian in origin and purpose. We are mis-framing the problem by asking, 'What is to be done about populism?' What we should be asking is, 'What has gone wrong with democracy?'

The causes of what has gone wrong vary from country to country and place to place, but several key factors are consistent. The first is the integrity and efficacy of the political class. Trust is in short supply, pushing citizens to look for alternatives not on the usual menu. Many pin their hopes on people who demonstrate greater 'authenticity', whether because they are plain-speaking and 'unspun', such as Corbyn and Sanders or, like Trump, Le Pen and Bolsonaro, have earned a reputation beyond the political fray, working in fields such as business, law or the military, where the ability to get things done and communicate well are prerequisites for success.

We are wrong to see this as a purely stylistic issue, a matter of repackaging political leadership. First, it is also a matter of what politics has become, under an increasingly intense scrutiny from the traditional media and the emergence of what John Keane calls 'monitory democracy', its calling to account by citizen reporters, whistle-blowers, informal groups and organisations such as WikiLeaks. The once-sharp separation between public and private realms is dissolving, with the result that elites find it harder to get away with the self-serving behaviours that earlier generations of politicians did. Populists of both the left and the right have made great play of the need for 'a new kind of politician', a politician who not only represents the people's needs and interests but also their requirement for clarity, integrity and honesty. This is not a one-way street. It is becoming ever more difficult for populists to control conditions such that they themselves escape scrutiny of a kind faced by their opponents. Populists will themselves be held accountable by the critique that brought them to power.

The second factor is regaining a sense that politics matters. Populism thrives when citizens feel powerless to alter the direction of their community. The Leave campaign found an unstoppable slogan in the Brexit referendum: 'Take Back Control'. This touched a nerve in the electorate, many of whom were convinced that the UK's membership of the European Union had, in return for uncertain economic benefits, ceded too much decision-making power. The irony is that arguably the most telling contribution the EU has made is in protecting its citizens from some of the worst impacts of globalisation: pressure on workers' rights, lowering of environmental standards and access to welfare; pressures that national governments are less well-equipped to withstand, given considerations of scale and capacity. The paradox of Brexit is that the UK may find itself having repatriated powers that are more hypothetical than real, accentuating people's sense of powerlessness, rather than addressing it.

This paradox highlights the complexity of the crisis, to which populism is but one response. It is far from straightforward to articulate what would enable citizens to feel that they have greater power or control. There are good reasons to think that framing the matter in these terms can lead to nowhere except a nostalgia for a time when democracy appeared 'meaningful'. The economist Dani Rodrik makes this point tellingly, when he notes that today's societies can have two of sovereignty, democracy and globalisation, but they cannot have all three, as the major powers arguably used to. Globalisation diminishes sovereignty and evacuates power from national parliaments to supra-national bodies and trans-national corporations; focusing on rebuilding democracy and public services might come at the expense of the inward investment brought by open markets and free movement of capital.

Without some change in the variables that underpin the question we may never be able to rediscover our sense of appropriating the political in a way that overcomes citizens' feeling of alienation. Some pin their hopes on revitalising politics at the city scale. Others hope that the Internet will encourage greater participation, due to the ease with which citizens can be connected to decision-making processes, which may in turn reduce citizens' sense of distance or alienation from their system of governance. Democracy is not a static entity. It evolves, morphs, shifts shape. It must, to keep its citizens' affection.

A third factor is insecurity. Insecure citizens are more likely to look beyond the mainstream for solutions to the issues that confront them. Compared to earlier generations, those issues are piling up: access to social services, precarious employment, automation, climate change, the pressures caused by displacement, migration and war. There are no easy solutions to any of these issues. Indeed, some now appear to have an almost existential dimension, literally a matter of the human species' existence, which feeds the sense that populism is a politics for the 'end of times'. Does it have to be like this? Is politics beyond redemption, lost to a discourse of outsiders forever complaining about the 'inside'?

The scale of the issues driving us towards the 'populisation' of democratic politics is considerable. This is not the same as saying that we are doomed to either an authoritarian future or the denigration of democracy. Populism is a politics of insiders and outsiders, of elites confronted by people who feel they have a better, more redemptive message, or a better grasp of the needs of the people, the community, the nation. Another contrary suggestion is that populism may revive a sense of politics as more than just a rotation of elites or a pendulum swing between parties that increasingly resemble each other, as far as many citizens are concerned. It may reintroduce a sense of contingency to politics at a time when 'business as usual' or technocratic approaches seem to have us sleepwalking towards the end of times.

This is deeply unsettling. Change, we are constantly reminded, often is. But it may be that populism's unsettling of the established political order, and the established way of doing things, represents an opportunity as well as a threat. My constant refrain in this book has been that we cannot understand the emergence of populist movements and parties without understanding the concept of crisis, in particular the crisis of democracy. This suggests that left to itself, democracy will not find the resources to climb out of the void into which politics has fallen. It won't help us escape the sense of politics as a monotone mediatised spectacle, increasingly distant from our lives and impervious to the needs and interests of our communities. It won't re-energise citizens into participating in and engaging with the democratic process. What is needed is a call for a return to the concept of democracy as a commons, as a political system whose unique property is that it belongs to anyone and everyone, to the *demos*, to the people.

Under contemporary conditions, such a call has an undeniably populist air. It suggests that representatives and represented have become disconnected, that elites hold sway and that people have been ignored. It's populist because we have allowed ourselves to be convinced that a democracy of, by and for the people is a pipe dream rather than a description of democracy's vocation. A populism focused on the renewal of democracy may indeed be an unsettling prospect, but if this is what is needed to halt its slow downward spiral into the void, it will be a price worth paying.

Acknowledgements

This book was written over the course of 2018, a period during which I was on leave from the University of Sydney. So my first note of thanks is to my employer for giving me the time to concentrate on writing. Thanks as well to Ben Moffitt, a former PhD student of mine who wrote a very fine thesis on populism, subsequently published by Stanford. Without those discussions over several years on the topic of populism I don't think I would have been equipped or energised to write my own book on the topic. Thanks as well to Aidan Anderson and Gianluca Scattu, two more of my PhD students, for commenting on a full draft of the manuscript.

I'd like to thank the numerous colleagues around Australia who invited me to give a paper on some or other aspect of the populism story. They include Duncan McDonnell, Haig Patapan and colleagues at Griffith; Paul Muldoon and the Politics Department at Monash; Stephen Slaughter, Benjamin Isakhan and colleagues at Deakin; Dave Marsh, Henrik Bang and IGPA at Canberra University which hosted a symposium on populism in 2017. The same year I was honoured to be invited to give a plenary address on populism at the Australian Political Studies Association in Melbourne. I was also delighted to give a paper in the legendary after-dinner slot at Oxford Political Thought. I learned a great deal from these talks and thank the participants at each for helping me to clarify my own thoughts on the topic.

I am pleased to acknowledge the key role of my friend and colleague John Keane, who does so much to keep many of the issues raised in this book on the boil for the rest of us at Sydney.

I've enjoyed and benefited from the countless events, seminars and workshops he's organised (with thanks also to colleagues at the Sydney Democracy Network) and look forward to many more as we try to make sense of these times. One of the more memorable events was the hosting of Nadia Urbinati for a set of lectures and talks around the theme of populism. It was wonderful to spend time with this formidable scholar of modern and contemporary politics and I learned a great deal from our conversations.

I also owe a considerable debt to Ramón Feenstra of the University of Jaume I, Castellón with whom I have undertaken fieldwork in Spain every year since 2013. Without his help and assistance I would never have been able to see at close hand the birth of 'outsider' movements and parties of a kind discussed in this text.

I'd also like to thank the team at Oneworld, especially Jon Bentley-Smith who, along with an anonymous expert reader, gave me a great deal of excellent feedback on an initial draft and in Jon's case on subsequent versions as well.

Finally, being marooned at home for much of the period whilst writing I learned to rely on Labancz for coffee, cakes and company, whilst the folks at Egg of the Universe and Velofix have kept me clear of mind and reasonably fit of body. Ben Triefus has sat and listened to my dubious theories over $5 schooners with barely a murmur of dissent and provided welcome company for the obligatory Sunday cycling jaunt. As ever, my greatest debt is to Véronique and the family for keeping me from going mad at the state of politics and the world more generally.

Further reading

Blyth, M. 'Global Trumpism', https://www.youtube.com/watch?v=Bkm2Vfj42FY&t=401s

Canovan, M. 1981. *Populism*. London, Junction Books.

Crouch, C. 2004. *Post-Democracy*. Cambridge, Polity.

Davis, E. 2018. *Post-Truth: Why We Have Reached Peak Bullshit And What We Can Do About It*. London, Little, Brown.

Flinders, M. 2012. *Defending Politics: Why Democracy Matters in the Twenty-First Century*. Oxford, Oxford University Press.

Fukuyama, F. 2016. 'American Political Decay or Renewal? The Meaning of the 2016 Election', *Foreign Affairs*, 95(4).

Galston, W. A. 2018. *Anti-Pluralism: The Populist Threat to Liberal Democracy*, New Haven CN, Yale University Press.

Goodhart, D. 2017. *The Road to Somewhere: The Populist Revolt and the Future of Politics*. Oxford, Oxford University Press.

Hay, C. 2007. *Why We Hate Politics*. Cambridge, Polity.

Judis, J. B. 2016. *The Populist Explosion. How the Great Recession Transformed American and European Politics*. New York, Columbia Global Reports.

Keane, J. 2009. *The Life and Death of Democracy*. London and New York, Simon and Schuster.

Laclau, E. 2005. *On Populist Reason*. London, Verso.

Mair, P. 2013. *Ruling the Void: The Hollowing of Western Democracy*. London, Verso.

Morozov, E. 2012. *The Net Delusion: The Dark Side of Internet Freedom*. London, Penguin.

Moffitt, B. *The Global Rise of Populism: Performance, Political Style and Representation*. Stanford CA, Stanford University Press.

Mouffe, C. and Í. Errejón. 2016. *Podemos: In the Name of the People*. London, Lawrence & Wishart.

Mounk, Y. 2018. *The People vs Democracy: Why our Freedom is in Danger and How to Save It*. Cambridge MA, Harvard University Press.

Mudde, C. and C. R. Kristobal. *Populism: A Very Short Introduction*. Oxford, Oxford University Press.

Müller, J-W. 2016. *What is Populism?* Philadelphia, University of Pennsylvania Press.

Norris, P. 2018. *Cultural Backlash and the Rise of Populism: Trump, Brexit and the Rise of Authoritarian Populism*. Cambridge, CUP.

Oliver, C. 2017. *Unleashing Demons: The Inside Story of Brexit*. London, Hodder.

Peston, R. 2018. *WTF*. London, Hodder.

Richards, S. 2018. *The Rise of The Outsiders: How Mainstream Politics Lost its Way*. London, Atlantic Books.

Shipman, T. 2017. *All Out War: The Full Story of How Brexit Sank Britain's Political Class*. London, Collins.

Taggart, P. 2000. *Populism*. Milton Keynes, Open University Press.

Tormey, S. 2015. *The End of Representative Politics*. Cambridge, Polity.

Vance, J. D. 2016. *Hillbilly Elegy: A Memoir of a Family and a Culture in Crisis*. New York, Harper.

Index